The Children & Have I None

Edward Bond is widely regarded as the greatest living British dramatist. These two plays are written with the austere language and haunting imagery for which he is famous. Both plays are set in the future and are concerned, not with sci-fi technology, but with our emotions, asking 'How will we live then?'

The Children

A disturbed mother sends her son on a bizarre errand which has fatal consequences. Leaving home, he embarks on a journey with his friends. Encountering evil, destruction and eventually compassion, he is drawn into a world that is changed for ever.

Have I None

A woman sitting alone hears a constant knocking at the door, but no one is there. Her husband returns and tells her of an extraordinary meeting with an old woman found roaming in a ruined part of the city. Then a stranger comes to the door, like a visitor from an earlier, lost world. What follows is tragic and absurdly funny until both seem to melt into a strange, hallucinatory vision of the future.

Edward Bond was born and educated in London. His plays include *The Pope's Wedding* (Royal Court Theatre, 1962), *Saved* (Royal Court, 1965), *Early Morning* (Royal Court, 1968), *Lear* (Royal Court, 1971), *The Sea* (Royal Court, 1973), *The Fool* (Royal Court, 1975), *The Woman* (National Theatre, 1978), *Restoration* (Royal Court, 1981), *Summer* (National Theatre, 1982), *The War Plays* (RSC at the Barbican Pit, 1985), *In the Company of Men* (Paris, 1992; RSC at the Barbican Pit, 1996), *At the Inland Sea* (toured by Big Brum Theatre-in-Education, 1995), *Coffee* (Rational Theatre Company, Cardiff and London, 1996) ... by Big Brum Theatre-in-Ed... ...enty-first

Century (published 1998 and produced in Paris, 2000), *The Children* (Classworks, Cambridge, 2000) and *Have I None* (toured by Big Brum Theatre-in-Education, 2000); also *Olly's Prison* (BBC2 Television, 1993), *Tuesday* (BBC Schools TV, 1993) and *Chair* (BBC Radio 4, 2000). His *Theatre Poems and Songs* were published in 1978 and *Poems* 1978–1985 in 1987. *Selections from the Notebooks of Edward Bond (Volume One: 1959–1980)* was published in 2000.

Edward Bond

The Children
&
Have I None

Methuen

Methuen 2000

1 3 5 7 9 10 8 6 4 2

First published in Great Britain in 2000
by Methuen Publishing Limited,
215 Vauxhall Bridge Road, London SW1V 1EJ

Copyright © 2000 Edward Bond

Edward Bond has asserted his rights under the Copyright, Designs
and Patents Act, 1988, to be identified as the author of this work

Methuen Publishing Limited Reg. No. 3543167

A CIP catalogue record for this book
is available from the British Library

ISBN 0 413 75630 0

Typeset by MATS, Southend-on-Sea, Essex

Printed and bound in Great Britain by
Cox & Wyman Ltd, Reading, Berkshire

Caution

Contents

For the pupils and staff of Manor Community College, Cambridge

The Children

A play to be acted by young people and two adults

CHILD: 'O help, help!
Where can I go to escape?'

Medea, Euripides

The Children was first presented by Classworks Theatre on 11 February 2000 at Manor Community College, Cambridge. The parts of the children were played by pupils from the College. The complete cast was as follows:

Joe	Darryl Griffiths
Jill	Lisa Fishpool
Stranger	Paul Carrig
Mum	Toni Midlane
Man	Mark Entwhistle (Cambridge) and Mark Laurie (tour)
Matt	Simon Gates
Ron	Adrian Maples-Kendrick
Adam	Luke Howlett
Don	Mark Smith
Marvin	Liam Osborne
Stacey	Laura Knights
Lisa	Karman Fowell
Tasha	Claire Stearn
Becca	Amy Carpenter
Gemma	Amy Davison
Naomi	Jenna Leonard
Paul	Ben Waters
Frank	Edward Carmody

Director Claudette Bryanston
Project Manager Barry A. E. Richardson
Designers Idit Nathan, Jo Hennessey
Lighting Designer Chetna Kapacee
ASM Sabrina Farrow
Technical Crew Carl Betson, Dan Upchurch
Backstage Kathy Thorpe, Gemma Jakes, Rachel Marsh, Amy Gates, Hayley Truesdale

Note
The Children initially toured to seventeen venues. The parts of **Mum** and **Man** (which should be performed as they are printed here) were played throughout the whole tour by the same actors, but for each new venue there was a different cast

of young people. The young people should perform their roles as they are printed in Scenes One, Two, Four, Eleven and Twelve. In all other scenes they should create their own parts, guided by the situations and words given to them in the text.

Sixteen young people performed in the first production. In further productions the number may be increased or decreased and the gender of the roles may be changed. Peterborough (the town named in Scenes Five and Six) may be changed to an appropriate local town.

One

Abandoned lot by a railway line.
Dusk.

Joe *comes on. He carries a stuffed puppet. It is about half his size. It is dressed in a brightly coloured jacket, dark grey trousers, white shirt, striped tie and brown shoes. Its clothes suggest school uniform.*

Joe Late. Dark soon. This used to be allotments. That's what the little sheds were for. They're falling down. They say they're haunted. Got spiders in them. (*Points.*) Railway line.

Don't cry. Shouldn't have brought you with me today. Brought you because you cried. Now you're crying even more. Are you afraid? You don't like the dark. You'll be all right for one night. Are you hungry? I'll bring you some sweets in the morning. What sweets shall I bring you?

My tea'll be cold. Mum'll be on the warpath. She's waiting to go out. If you could walk we'd go back together. I'd drop you at your front door. Stand out in the street. Hear them shout at you inside for being late. We'd laugh about it in the morning. That used to be my jacket. Passed it on to you when I grew out of it. Still put my things in the pockets. Secret hiding place. Don't cry. If you cry I won't bring you the sweets. Oh dear! — now he'll cry even more. What sweets d'you want? I'll buy them with Mum's fag money. Say I lost it. She won't believe me. I don't care.

Why do I drag you around? You get me into trouble. Didn't go to school today because of you. Mum won't have you in the house any more. She'd send you to the jumble sale. 'That's where you won him in the raffle. Take him back. Make some money out of him.' Or chuck you in the rubbish when I'm at school. You stare at me. If you were real we'd quarrel. That'd be that! I'd tell you to get lost! I even have to do your talking for you. Sometimes I hear myself talk and think it's you. Anyone listening now would think I'm mad. It's got to stop! I'm too old for you! You're nothing! A puppet stuffed with packing!

It's not my fault you're not real. You're better off like that. No exams. No errands. 'Clear that up. I'm not tidying your room!' What sweets d'you want? I don't even know what your favourites are. I give you mine. I just supposed they're yours.

(*Doesn't look up.*) When it's getting dark the sky's dirty. Streaky. It's forgot to wash its face. I told you everything I didn't tell anyone else. It used to be such fun with you. It's not any more. I have to tell you the truth. I always have. No lies. I brought you here to get rid of you. You have to learn to be on your own. You can't. You'll never be able to look after yourself. That's why you can't let me go. You've got my comb.

He takes a comb from the puppet's pocket. Combs his hair. Puts the comb in his own pocket.

I'll have to kill you.

He goes out. He comes back with a brick.

You won't feel it. Cheerio. (*He drops the brick on the puppet's head.*) Shut your eyes. Be dead.

He goes out. He comes back with a brick. He stops, wanders a few steps.

Anything goes wrong in our house Mum hits me. Don't know why. Am I supposed to change the world? (*He goes to the puppet. Looks at it.*) Got dirty green on your face. Off the brick. If I had a torch there'd be blood where I walk between you and the bricks.

He drops the brick on the puppet's head. He goes out and comes back with a brick. He drops it on the puppet's head.

That's enough. Won't leave you here when it's done. Stream at the back. Allotment holders got water from it for their plants. Mucky. Full of crates and trollies. Won't throw you in the water. Lay you on the bank. Out of sight. The cats and dogs won't get you. If you turned into a ghost you'd hear the stream run when it rained. No ghosts. There's nothing like that.

He picks up the puppet. Half-hugs and playfully half-swings it from side to side.

You're nearly dead. One more.

He puts down the puppet. Starts to go. Suddenly stops.

Has to be! (*Runs back to the puppet. Picks up a brick. Hits the puppet with the brick.*) Has to be! Can't give you away to someone who doesn't care! (*Hits the puppet with the brick.*) Can't leave you on a bus! (*Hits the puppet with the brick.*) Someone might find you – who didn't humiliate you! (*Hits the puppet with the brick.*) Didn't hurt you! (*Hits the puppet with the brick.*) I can't! You're mine! (*Pause.*) Phew! (*Stands. Looks at his hand.*) Muck. (*Brushes his hands together.*) Dark. Mum'll rave. She's going out with her new boyfriend.

Joe *takes hold of the puppet by the leg and drags it out behind him.*

Two

Home.
Later.

Mother *sits on a wooden chair. Broods. A noise at the front door. She perks up.*

Mother (*calls*)   You back dear?

Joe *comes in.*

Joe (*awkward*)   Sorry I'm late.

Mother   O I don't call this late. I expect you've been with your mates. Nice time?

Joe (*confused*)   Well.

Mother   Enjoy yourself your age. There isn't much enjoyment later.

Joe (*misunderstanding*)   I stopped you going out.

Mother   Didn't really want to. Didn't have the energy to dress up. Hard day at work. You gave me an excuse to stay in. Your tea's in the micro. Just needs switching on.

Joe *starts to go to the other room. Stops.*

Joe   I lost your fag money.

Mother   O? How?

Joe   Lost it.

Mother (*irritated*)   You can't have 'lost it'! Look in your pockets.

Joe   Have.

Mother   Look again. People don't just lose things. I had to work for that. I don't sit in a chair all day or make myself a nuisance hanging round bus shelters.

Joe   I'll switch the micro –

Mother   Don't walk away when I'm talking to you! (*She calms herself.*) Well. I smoke too much anyway. Won't hurt me to go without till morning. I suppose. Give my lungs a rest.

Joe (*mumbles*)   Sorry – I'll go and switch the –

Mother   I've got a favour to ask. Take your coat off. I told you before not to wear it round the house.

Joe *goes out into the other room.*

Mother (*calls*)   And hang it up properly.

Joe *comes back without his jacket.*

Mother   Promise me you'll do something.

Joe   Can't promise till I know what it –

Mother   I'm your mother. If I ask you to promise me you shouldn't raise objections. You should *want* to do it.

Joe   OK.

Mother   Don't be flippant. I don't often ask for anything.

Joe   What is it?

Mother   Don't change the subject. You can be damned annoying when you try. I'm not telling you till you promise. You'll have to show you're willing before I can take it any further. I can't involve you otherwise. It wouldn't be right.

Joe   I'll pay the fag money back. I lost it on the –

Mother (*annoyed*)   Stop talking about that blasted fag money!
It's nothing to do with that! I try to be serious and you just
pass silly remarks. I ask for help and all you can say is 'What is
it?' Who else can I turn to? Not your father – even if I knew
where he was. I do what I can. Go to work. Keep the home
together. Provide the meals. Send you out decent. Then you
turn your back on me when I ask you to –

Joe   I can't do it unless I know what it is!

Mother   Go and switch the micro on. Have your meal. You
make me weary. I shouldn't have asked. Might've known what
the answer would be. You're turning out just like your father.

Joe *turns to go.*

Mother   Where you going?

Joe   Turn the micro –

Mother   You go when I say, not before.

Joe   You just told me to switch the –

Mother   Don't answer back! Save your lip for outside where
it's appreciated. I'm upset because I don't know which way to
turn. You can see the state I'm in. You can't give up even one
meal to listen.

Joe   Sorry.

Mother   What's that supposed to mean? If you knew what
you've done this evening you'd be sorry for the rest of your
life. Any normal boy would put his arms round his mother
and say 'I'll do it Mum. Anything!' It was a mistake to ask.
You've got your own problems. I should never have involved
you in mine. (*Sudden low anger.*) But I'd like to know where my
fag money went! What shop that was lost in . . .

Joe   Tell me, Mum.

Mother   I can't. Not if you begged me. So don't waste your
breath asking. I'd have to have your solemn word first. At least

I'd know you were grown up enough to understand what loyalty is. Your father never did.

Joe   I'll do it.

Mother   Too late. It's easy to offer when you don't know what it is. When you don't have to carry the responsibility.

Joe   I promise.

Mother   You expect me to believe that after the way you've just behaved?

Joe   I'll do it.

Mother   I don't want you to. I won't give you the chance.

Silence.

Mother   You see the mess you've got us into? If I don't tell you now I'll never hear the last of it. You won't be fit to live with. I've seen too much of that in the past. And if I do tell you you'll say I forced you so you couldn't get out of it! I hope you're satisfied.

Joe   Mum.

Mother   Is that your solemn word?

Joe   Yes.

Mother   As God's my witness I didn't want to tell you. I've no choice. If I don't you'll say I don't trust you even when you give your solemn word!

Joe   Mum, I don't understand any more. Tell me and I'll have my tea.

Mother   O you poor kid you're hungry. I forget you're still a child. Put your arms round me. Give me a hug. I feel as if I've forced you. What I'm asking isn't for myself – it's for *us*.

Joe *puts his arms round her.*

Joe   Don't cry Mum. Please.

Mother   There. You know how to get your way with me. I have to admit it, you twist me round your little finger. You're all I've got in the world. I wouldn't go on without you.

Joe (*scared*)   No no don't start it again! I don't want to hear it! – tablets – throw yourself off a bridge – (*Sudden panic.*) Oh no, Mum! – you don't want me to help you to – I can't! –

Mother   No no it's not –

Joe   No – no – no –

Mother   – no – no – I couldn't! Couldn't! No – I'd never put you through that. If ever I kill myself I wouldn't tell you. You'd have to come home one day and find me on the floor. If you do this – for *us* – our suffering's over. (*She calms herself, straightens her dress.*) You haven't got a fag on you? I know what you kids get up to. I'm dying for a ciggie . . . (*No answer. She reaches for him.*) Don't pull away. I can tell you when you're close. Am I such a bad mother? – my own son thinks I'm asking him to help me do away with myself . . . poor kid.

Joe (*becoming calm*)   Tell me Mum.

Mother   I'll give you an address. A house on the new estate. You can't miss it. They've only finished one street. The rest's still mud. It's got a mauve door.

Joe   Mauve.

Mother   Go in daylight hours. Make sure you know the house. Go back in the dark. Set it on fire. Burn it down. Your father left his old cans in the shed – done some good for a change. Carry the petrol in that. The workmen leave wood and stuff lying round. It's all flammable. They're so lazy they probably left the petrol for the machines. Borrow that.

Joe   Whose house is it?

Mother   You read of houses set on fire. Offices. Sports pavilions. It's easy. I can't answer any questions. Don't pry. The less you know the better. There are secrets that can't be revealed. I'm not at liberty. Make sure it's the house with the mauve door.

Joe   Why? Who lives there? I won't ask anything else.

Mother   I'd do it but it's against the law. It's not *wrong*. If you knew the circumstances I'm shielding you from – you'd say burning wasn't drastic enough! I've thought about it for us. If you were caught – at your age they don't expect any better. They'd put it down to an absentee father. You'd only be sent away for a little while. I'd visit you. If *I* did it they'd send me away for years. You'd be alone. First you've got no father, then you'd be deprived of a mother – just at the age when you need parental guidance. Your life would be ruined. This will keep us together. Bring us closer. You could come in all hours – I'd never complain. (*Playfully wags her finger at him.*) And you could never answer me back – you'd be too scared I'd tell the police what you'd been up to! (*Little chuckle.*) I'm glad I spoke. Did you hang your jacket up?

Joe   Mum –

Mother   Look at me! – forgetting the tea of this starving boy! I'll put the micro on.

Mother *goes out into the other room.*

Mother (*off*)   When you're older I'll tell you more. You wouldn't understand now.

Joe (*half loud, practising*)   I won't do it.

Silence. **Mother** *comes back.*

Mother   Wash your hands before you get up to table.

Joe   I can't do it.

Mother   It's too late to cadge a fag from next door. (*Slight pause.*) Of course if I thought like you you wouldn't be here. You'd've ended up in the pedal bin in an abortion clinic. I could've abandoned you when your father abandoned me. You can't always be a child. You grow up. Have to make hard choices. They can't teach you that at school. Some children inherit money from their parents – I inherited poverty from mine. Babies cry? – your mother cried herself to sleep every night. I scrimped and scraped for every penny. I don't ask for gratitude or recompense. But if you love me you'd do what I ask.

Joe   You don't know what you're doing.

Mother (*flaring*)   Don't you cheek me! Don't tell me I don't know! Don't know? You little devil – what d'you know about anything? After all I've been through I know! You think I'd put you – with your moods – under an obligation if I didn't have to? Perhaps *I'm* the one under an obligation! Perhaps I'm doing it for someone else! You don't have to be my whole life, you know! I've got a life on the other side of that door! And this was the boy who gave his mother his solemn word! I'll tell you this – and I was never more sober in my life when I say it: that house'll be burnt!

Joe   You'll get us into trouble!

Mother   No more! Enough! Go and swallow your meal if you can!

Joe goes out into the other room.

Mother (*calls*)   From now on this'll be a house of silence. O I'll talk to you: 'Shut the door – don't be late – wash your hands.' But it's the last time I'll tell you anything that matters to me. A stone'd say more than I will. You won't like that.

Joe comes back. He is putting on his jacket.

Mother   You're not going on to the streets this time of night giving me a bad name.

Joe goes out.

Mother (*calls*)   I exposed myself to you. I regret it. (*Goes to the door and shouts.*) If your father'd asked you you'd do it!

Sound of the street door closing.

Mauve door. (*She sits on the chair.*) How could . . . the insult, insult. (*Suddenly slowly and carefully.*) I wonder if he's gone to do it now? (*Off, bell.*) Micro.

She goes out into the other room.

Three

Abandoned lot by a railway line.
Morning.

Joe *sits huddled alone.*

Jill *comes in.* **Joe** *looks up.*

Jill (*calls over her shoulder*)   Here! Said he would be.

Joe's **Friends** *begin to come in. They are about his age.*

Friends   Called at your place this morning.
Your mum said you'd left early.

Joe   Didn't go home last night.

Friends   Where were you?

Joe   Here.

Friends   All night?
What for?

Joe   My mum's in trouble.

Friends   Wow! – tell us!
What trouble?

Joe   It's serious. You mustn't tell. I only know a bit of it. She
wants me to burn a house.

Friends   Burn it?
Burn it down?
Whose house?

Joe   New estate.

Friends   She serious?
He's having you on! – or she is!
What for?

Joe   She wouldn't say. She's desperate about something – or
she'd've gone to the police. I think she's in danger.

Friends   New estate! – I'd burn the lot!
If it was my mum I'd set fire to *her* –

It's not funny.
– but I'd do it out the back: my room's just been decorated.
Shut it!
You pile rubbish up against the door.
Soak rags in petrol. Push them through the letter box.
Light a match – drop it in –
And run!
(*Low, warning.*) Hang about – kid watching through the
fence.
(*Calls.*) What you want?
Sod off spy!
Read the notice: 'trespassers prosecuted'.
Can't read!

A **Stranger** *comes in. He is dressed in the same way as the* **Friends**.

Friends   Who're you?
This is ours. You're not invited.

Stranger   Exploring.

Friends   Go and explore somewhere else!
You're not from round here.

Stranger   New estate. The other kids'll move in when it's
finished.

Friends   My mum says you've got big executive kitchens.
You posh?

Stranger   Don't know.

Friends   Your people must be posh in them big houses!
Rolling in it!
Have to pay to join our club.
He's not joining – no new-estaters!
Bash you!
War!

Stranger   My dad says only wineos and dossers come to this
dump!

Friends   Hop it!
Tie him on the rail-line.

The **Stranger** *runs off.*

Stranger (*off*)   My dad says don't play with that riff-raff. You'll catch their stink!

They duck.

Friends   Little bugger chucking stones!
Skin him!
We'll throttle you! – tell your dad that!
Murder the little sod!

Some of them chase after the **Stranger**.

Leave him!
Do him later!

The others drift back.

. . . sod dodged off . . .
. . . wants thumping . . .

They stare at **Joe** *in silence.*

Friend   She's got to tell you why.

Joe *shrugs.*

Friend   What'll you do?

Joe (*slight pause*)   It's only a house.

Friends   He's going to do it . . . !
Phew! I'm not getting involved!
The cops'll question all of us.
They'll make us talk – they're trained. What chance we got?
One of us'll talk.
Then we all will!
If we say we knew they'll say we're as bad as he is for not stopping him.
I wasn't here!
Nor me!
The kid saw you!
I'll break his neck!
Big help! – *he's* up for arson and *we're* up for murder!

Joe *stands. Goes out.*

Friends (*calls*)   Oi! Don't bugger off!
(*calls*)   Haven't finished with you yet!
(*calls*)   Your mum gets these crazy ideas you wanna keep
them to yourself!
(*calls*)   Runs in the family!
(*calls*)   His mum's a –
Shut up!

Joe *comes back with the puppet.*

Friends   You still got that?
It's bashed in!

Joe   Did it with a brick. If your mum asked you, you'd do it.
Can't go home if I don't. It'd be hell. If the cops ask I'll say I
didn't do it. So I couldn't have told you I was going to! You're
in the clear. We were on the allotments – rowed with the kid –
and that's all. If they ask what we we're doing here: chucking
bricks at this.

Jill *goes out.*

Friend   You're not to blame. She made you do it.

Joe (*Shakes head*)   If I do it I'm to blame. She asked me for
help. I can't make it worse for her. I'll be all right.

Friends   If only the little sod hadn't chucked stones!
They'll say we burnt the house for revenge!
You said 'It's war!'
I never – it was him!
I never said it!
Yes you did!
No I never!
Shut it! – you sound like kids.

Jill *comes back with a greengrocer's carton filled with bricks. She drops
the bricks on the ground.* **Joe** *sets the puppet upright.*

Joe   We promise not to tell. Brick him – and swear we won't.

Friend   It's a pact! We swear to each other.

Hesitation. One of them takes a brick.

Friends   What do I say?
I swear to – (*Stops. Shrugs.*)
Keep my mouth shut. I promise the others.
(*Drops brick on puppet.*) I swear to keep my mouth shut.

The puppet sinks and falls back. For a moment they stare in silence. Then they rush to the bricks.

Friends   Brick it! Brick it! Brick it!

They take turns to drop bricks on the puppet. Then they begin to throw them, jostle and push.

Friends   Brick it! Brick it! Brick it!
Swear! Keep your mouth shut! Promise the others!
You had your go!
(*Imitating the puppet.*) Ow! Ouch! That hurt!

Naomi   I can't!

They drag **Naomi** *towards the puppet.*

Friends   Brick! Brick! Brick! In her hand! Make her!

They force a brick into **Naomi**'s *hand. Push her to the puppet. She drops the brick on the ground.*

Brick it! Brick it! Brick it!

They force **Naomi**'s *hand round a brick. They form a circle round the puppet. They push her into the circle. Behind the screen of bodies they force her to beat the puppet with the brick.*

Brick! Brick! Brick! Swear! Swear!

Naomi   Swear!

Friends   Keep my mouth shut!

Naomi   Shut!

Friends   The others!

Naomi   Others!

They stand back. Look at the puppet.

Friends   It hurt.
That's all we could do for Joe.

They start to go.

Friends   Look out for cops.
And the kid.

They go. The puppet lies under heaped bricks. **Joe** *comes back. He kneels by it. He takes a sweet packet from his own pocket. Puts a sweet in the puppet's mouth. It falls out.*

Joe   Take it! I brought the sweets! I said I would! (*He crams the sweet packet into the puppet's pocket.*) Take it! Why is it always a mess? Always the same? What do they want? What do they want? (*In despair, beyond tears.*) Look at yourself!

He clears the bricks, throwing them to the side.

Look at yourself! Look at yourself! (*He looks round for the last brick.*) Look at yourself!

He has cleared the bricks. He picks up the puppet by the leg. Drags it behind him.

Look at yourself!

Joe *goes.*

Four

Home.
Night.

Mother *waits tensely by the window. Arms crossed. She hears the sound of the front door. She hurries to the chair. Sits. Composes herself.*

Mother (*calls*)   What's the excuse this time? Becoming a regular habit. Haven't your mates got homes to go to?

Joe *comes in.*

Joe   It's OK.

Mother   I can't remember if I told you? – I'm changing my job. Handed in my notice today. I'm not appreciated. Look round for something better. Not any old thing. We might have to move further out.

Joe   It's OK.

Mother   Is it? I'll be the judge of that. Look at the state of you! – go round like a scruff to shame me. (*Sniffs.*) You smell. Hope you haven't been smoking? Bad enough one smoker in the family. I can't afford two on the habit.

Joe   It's OK.

Mother   Where've you been? You're a real worry to me sometimes.

Joe (*realising*)   O – nothing.

Mother   Wash your hands.

Joe *goes out to the other room.*

Mother (*half-trance, to herself*)   Mauve door . . . their whole attitude's in that. The dishonesty of it! Not mauve now . . . I struck a blow.

Joe *comes in.*

Mother   Did you hang the towel on the rail? –

Joe   Hid in a ditch in the garden.

Mother   – not drop it on the floor as per usual for me to pick up.

Joe   They'd been laying drains. I waited. Thought it had gone out. Went back. Looked through the window. Nothing. Then a light flickered up in the hall. Saw the room full of black smoke – turning and turning.

Mother   I hope you haven't been getting into mischief.

Joe   I broke a window. Air went in: whoosh!

Mother   You been watching videos again?

Joe   I've got to tell you what it – I burnt the house.

Mother   I wish I understood you sometimes. My own son's a riddle to me.

Joe   Went back. Hid in the ditch till I was sure. Kept some petrol in the can in case. It took off: whaahhh! Ran. Tripped in the ditch. On a rat. Splashed petrol. My hands. Jeans.

Mother   O God! – the fire engines I heard – was that – ?

Joe   It's OK.

Mother   You burnt a – ? You're pretending – to scare me –

Joe   It's OK.

Silence. **Mother** *stands, goes to* **Joe** *and hits him across the face.*

Mother   You wicked boy!

Joe   Mauve door.

Mother   You burnt a house?

Joe   You said!

Silence. **Mother** *hits him across the face again.*

Mother   You wicked, wicked, wicked boy!

Joe   Pretend tomorrow! – have to tell you what it was like in –

Mother   Stop it! Stop it! – He stinks of petrol! He must be telling the truth! Splashed when he tripped in the – ! O God, he's treading it in my floor! If the police come how could I protect you? If I said you'd been here with me all night they'd say 'What about the petrol on the floor?' Take your shoes off! Give me your jeans to – ! Get in the bath! I'll wash everything! No they'd still know! They detect everything! I was with Mrs Pierce all evening. I'll get her to say I was here – she phoned at half-ten when the fire engines – and while she was on I had to ask you something – she can vouch for that – which proves you were *here* – you couldn't have done it! (*She goes to strike* **Joe** *again but doesn't.*) You wicked boy!

Joe   Mum you told me to do – !

Mother   Stop it! Stop it! Don't ever say that! I'll wash your mouth out in disinfectant! Told you to burn a house? What mother would tell her child to do that. She'd be a monster! No one would believe you!

Joe   It doesn't matter.

Mother   Doesn't matter? You burn a house – then make a wicked accusation – and say it doesn't matter? What's the world coming to? Where did we go wrong with the young? I should take you to the police! Now! Let you suffer the consequence of your actions! I'm a fool to protect you. Did anyone – were you seen? Oh God, he's still got his shoes on! Off! Off! Treading in his filth! (**Joe** *tears off his shoes in panic.*) Burn them! Gimmee! I'll burn them! Security guards! – did they see? They put cameras in sites! Oh what a wicked wicked – I knew you were bad, but *this* – !

Joe (*panic*)   Mum you –

Mother   Don't you dare!

Joe   Mum!

Mother   Don't Mum me! I'm not your Mum! Don't come whining to me when they –

Doorbell.

Oh my God – it's started. It's coming to pieces.

Joe *turns to the door.*

Mother   Stay there! You're not ducking off under their arms! Then they'd know this is a guilty house!

Joe   We must –

Mother   They don't know we're in. Wait till they go. It might be about something else.

Joe   This late?

Mother   How did they know it was *this* house? You were

seen. Stupid wicked boy . . . ! I'll be sent to prison for not
keeping you under control!

Joe (*suddenly very tired*)   I'll answer it.

Doorbell.

Mother   In bed! They find you in your socks – !

Joe *goes out into the other room.* **Mother** *straightens her hair and
dress. Goes towards door.*

Mother (*calls*)   On my way.

Mother *sees* **Joe**'*s shoes on the floor. Snatches them up, goes out into
the next room. Doorbell.* **Mother** *comes back wrapped in a floral
dressing gown. Goes out to the front door. The sound of it opening.*

Mother (*off*)   This time of night? Come in. Next door'll
gossip if you stand on the doorstep.

Jill *comes in in street clothes. After a few moments the front door is heard
closing.* **Mother** *comes in.*

Mother   All their lights on. Heard the sirens. What do you
want?

Jill   See Joe Mrs Carter.

Mother   I'll take a message and give it to him in the
morning.

Jill   The fire –

Mother   We know there's a fire. You got me up to tell me
that?

Jill   Can I speak to Joe?

Mother   No. Bad enough fire engines racing up and
down. I'm not waking him a second time. Now if you don't
mind –

Jill   Someone was in the fire. Trapped.

Mother   I don't understand what you want to say.

Jill   Someone's dead.

A second's silence.

Mother (*short, humourless laugh*)   Dead. How stupid it is. Stupid. (*She sits in the chair. Calm.*) Thank you. I'll tell Joe in the morning. Can you see yourself out?

Joe *comes in. He has heard what* **Jill** *has said.*

Mother (*calmly*)   Imagine Joe – the fire engines we heard. Someone's burnt. Might be serious. Let's hope the ambulance service got there on time for once. Your friend came to tell you. Wasn't that kind of –

Joe (*to* **Mother**)   Dead.

Jill   On the landing. Trapped. A boy. Running with his clothes on fire.

Mother   Now – (*Stops.*) – I don't know your name?

Jill   Jill.

Mother   Jill – we mustn't exaggerate – we don't know any of the –

Joe   I thought the house was empty. I waited till –

Mother (*horrified*)   What are you saying? He's still asleep. He doesn't know what he – (*Explaining to* **Joe**.) There's been a fire Joe. Remember the sirens? They've given you a bad dream. Go back to bed. We'll get no sense out of you tonight.

Joe   I heard someone screaming. I thought it was next door giving the alarm.

Mother   He's suffered from his nightmares since his father left. We must – did you say *Jill*? – leave him or he gets upset. Go home – won't your parents be worried where you are? – or are they the modern sort? What were you doing out this late anyway? There's always mischief with you kids.

Joe (*to* **Mother**)   You've got to help me!

Mother   It's just rumour-rubbish she's picked up. Tittle-tattle. They enjoy grabbing the wrong end of the stick and beating everyone on the head with it. New estate? – some squatter moved in – on drugs – ~~burnt himself to death~~ –

Jill   A medic told the reporter.

Mother   I'll complain to your parents about you. Write to the school. (*To* **Joe**.) It's all right, I'll get rid of her. (*To* **Jill**.) You've got no right to come round here making yourself a nuisance.

Jill   You made him do it.

Mother (*horrified, to* **Joe**)   Have you been talking outside to – how could you! – gossiping about me to – ! (*To* **Jill**.) What else did he say? (*To* **Joe**.) Lies! Lies! Lies! Who else you told? Who else? It doesn't matter! If that little trollop knows everyone does! A poor dead boy! Not suffocated! Burnt! The worst way to go! On the landing! Now you see the difference between your games and the real world! Don't blame it on me! If I told you to do it, that's the first time you've done anything I've told you to!

Joe *goes out into the other room.*

Mother (*to* **Jill**)   His vivid imagination. The sirens confused him Jill – what a nice name! (*Calls.*) Tuck yourself in. I'll bring you a hot drink. (*To* **Jill**.) Did he mention any of this to anyone else?

Joe *comes back carrying his shoes.* **Mother** *is too preoccupied to notice. She looks out of the window.* **Joe** *puts on his shoes.*

Mother   The glow's died down already. Hardly worth the fire engines turning out. If you're in a fire it's your responsibility to keep calm – not get trapped on the landing. The school teaches you fire drill. These houses are just firewood waiting to go up. They shouldn't be allowed to build them. (*Sees* **Joe**.) You mustn't accuse your mother. A boy's been murdered. I sent my child out to do that? How could any mother survive it. They'd call her a monster. Even if it was true – if there was a particle of truth in it – you'd have to protect me. They make excuses if you're young. No one would make excuses for me. No one ever has. That's the story of my life. I know what the future would be . . . (*Breaks down.*) It'd never occur to me – never – you were talking about me on the streets. They'll pry and pry till they wear me down. They'll take everything – the few bits and pieces I've managed to hold on to. I wish I'd died in the fire! (*To* **Jill**.) I'm a good mother! I wouldn't let him do wrong! Make him help me to – I've forgotten your name? (*To* **Joe**.) If you did anything for me – it's because you love me! If you accuse me I'll deny it! It's the only way I can hold on to you! I won't let them take your love away from me! (*Wail.*) Don't betray me! (*Breaks down in incoherent tears. To* **Jill**.) Please. Tell him he'll regret it all his life. I'll kill myself! I mean it this time! (*She sees* **Joe** *is wearing his shoes.*) Why's he got his shoes on? Standing there! Take them off! Treading filth in my – He wants to give them evidence! Get me sent away! – Where are you going?

Joe   Out.

Mother   To tell your friends more lies?

Joe *and* **Jill** *start to leave.*

Mother   I forbid you to go! I'm ordering you! If you're seen out on the streets tonight – they'll pick you up! You go through that door over my dead body!

Joe *and* **Jill** *go out.*

Mother (*shouts*)   I won't be here when you come back!

The front door is heard opening and shutting.

Mother (*trying to control herself*)   What shall I do? Can't chase him through the streets. (*Panic.*) They've gone to the police! (*Rehearsing.*) I might have said something, as you do. We all say things officer. I'm certain I never meant –. As I told his teacher (which she'll corroborate) when he gets an idea in his head it's like prising nails out of solid iron . . . Mauve. Mauve. The insult. (*Looks round.*) I have nothing.

Mother *goes into the other room.*

Five

Abandoned lot by a railway line.
Morning.

Joe *sits alone. He is cold and hungry.*

Some of the **Friends** *come on.*

Friends   Said you'd be here again!
Been here all night?
The others are looking for you.
The police are searching the house. It's a wreck.
What you going to do?

Joe   Run away.

Friend   Where?

Joe   Where they can't find me.

Friends   You run the cops'll know you did it.
Go to them. Tell them your mother made you.

Jill *and the rest of the* **Friends** *come on.*

Friend   He's running away.

Joe   Been round my mother's?

Jill   Yes.

Joe   How is she?

Jill   Crying.

Friends   We're all suspects
The cops'll come to the school.
We'll tell them your mum made you do it.
They won't believe us.
Worse if they did – they'll want to know why we didn't stop
him.
Chriss!
They'll say if we didn't stop him we're as bad as he is.
I didn't know. Never told me.
Nor me.

I'm not telling the cops anything.
(*Laugh.*) You will! Who told them I smashed the car?
It was my dad's car!
Shut up! Don't start that!
(*To* **Joe**.) We'll go and collect your things.
Can't. His mum'd tell the police.
They'd follow you back here.
He can't go like that – (*To* **Joe**.) you need your things.

Jill   I'll go with you.

Joe   That's stupid. You'd mess your life up.

Jill   Messed it up already. Worse the longer I stay.

Slight pause.

Friends   A kid's dead. That's serious.
They'll clobber us.
We didn't know he'd be dead.
Nor did Joe!
We didn't think. *That's* why he's dead.
We're all to blame.
We're not! *They're* to blame. There wouldn't have been a fire if
his mother hadn't said.
If we don't get it in the neck for this they'll find something
else.

Jill (*to* **Joe**)   I'll come with you.

Friends   And me.
We should all go.
Shall we?
Least it's out of this dump!
Let's go! All of us!
When?
Now!
Fetch our things first.
No just go!
This is crazy!
Haven't fed my rabbits –
No one's going back!

– if I don't no one will.
They'd ask questions – then we've all had it.
Hope your family like rabbit pie.
Let's go!
Where?
North!
Peterborough!

Silence. They look at each other.

Their faces in the morning . . . !
Be a laugh.
Teach them a lesson.
Serves them right!
Joe? Can we? With you?

They stare at **Joe**. *He sits with his face in his hands.*

Joe   I can't manage it any more. My hands – stink of petrol
. . . I wouldn't be alone . . .

Behind them a **Man** *comes on slowly. He is tall and thin, his face is
white, his hair is matted. He wears a long black overcoat, dark trousers,
black boots and pearl-grey cloth gloves. He moves as if he does not see the
others. He stops, stares at the ground. Falls. The friends turn to look at
him. He lies completely still.*

Friend   Sloshed.

Joe *remains sitting. The others cluster round the* **Man**.

Friends   My old man drinks. Doesn't look like that.
Dead.
Chriss! – now we'll be blamed for that.
He's breathing.

They edge back cautiously. **Joe** *stands up to to watch.*

Friends   Look in his pockets.
Be empty – dosser.
Can't leave him here.
He'll be dead in the morning!
Sod him that's his fault! Leave him!
Let's go like we said!

Sod it! Sod it! – a tramp turns up and we're trapped.

They hesitate.

Take him till we meet someone – let them look after him.
Get a door from the sheds. Stretcher him on that.

Some of them go to fetch a door.

He's not from round here.
On his way through.
Think he heard what we were saying?
In his state?

The others have come back with a door.

Friends   My mum can't cope in her wheelchair. I do our
shopping – cooking –
What are neighbours for?
They don't help.
They'll have to. Why is it always us?
She'll break her heart.
A boy's dead. No one else'll help us. We have to stick together.
We're not chucking it in before we start!
Let's go! Let's go!

The **Man** *is lifted on to the door.*

Friends   Heavy! Not carrying this far!
Typical! – tramp who can't walk!

They go.

Six

Journey.
Evening a few days later.

Some of the **Friends** *come on.*

Friends   Must be an emergency.
You keep saying that.
Must be.

Can't. There was no explosion. No bodies.
No cars or lorries. Roads empty.
If there was an emergency they'd be choked.
No dogs. Not even dead ones.
No washing on the lines.
Everyone's vanished.
Weird.
I'm scared.
We saw some people going over a hill. We shouted. They
didn't stop.
Perhaps everyone's been moved to Peterborough.
Why?
Safety.
Scares me.

The rest of the **Friends** *come on with the door. The* **Man** *sleeps on it.*

Friends   See anyone?

Head shakes.

Take a rest. He's pulling my arms off.
Didn't wake up?

Head shakes.

If he doesn't eat he'll die.
I'm not going to his funeral. He's not our responsibility.
Should've left him. His mates'll be looking for him.
What mates? – everyone's vanished.
Where's the others?
Reccying Peterborough. (*Points.*) That's them coming back.

The **Man**'s *arm slips from the door.*

Friends   His arm!
His eyes are open.
Who are you?
Where you from?
D'you know where everyone's gone?
He can't hear.
D'you know what's going wrong?
Don't be scared.

We wanted to take you to a hospital.
Perhaps there'll still be one in Peterborough.

Joe *and the rest come in. They have a couple of sacks.*

Friends   Empty. No one.
Whole town deserted.
All of it?
Everywhere's deserted.
Now what do we do?

They stare at each other.

It's us. We're still back at the allotments. We're not here. We
imagined it.
Don't start that! We've got to keep our heads.
Look at that raw on my hands – carrying him. I didn't
imagine that!
He's the cause of it! If we dump him it'll all go back to normal.
I said don't start! How could one man control everything?
Get rid of him!

Joe   We can't leave him now! There's no one else. He'd die.

Friend   His eyes are shut.

One of them puts the **Man**'s *arm back under the pieces of blanket.*

Friends   What's in the sacks?
Tins. Grub.
Nicked from the empty houses.
Great! – a proper meal! I'm starving.
Could be contaminated.
Got to eat. There's nothing else.
Look – the street lights are coming on.

They gaze towards the town.

Automatic when it's dark.
Won't the power run out?
Wind farms keep feeding the grid.
We could go and live there.
Not me! You haven't seen it. Ghost town. Gives me the
creeps.

We've got to keep going till we come to people. They must be *somewhere*.
Let's find a place for the night and open the tins.
I can't carry him with my raw hands.
Give it here.

They start to carry out the **Man**.

Friend (*gazing at the town*)   All the empty streets lit up for nobody.

They go.

Seven

Journey.
Evening, a week later.

The **Friends** *come on together. One carries a sack. Others carry the* **Man** *on an old army stretcher. It has short legs and wheels that are too small for distances but can be used to manoeuvre it. The* **Man** *sleeps. He is covered with bits of old blankets. One of them is rolled up for a pillow.*

Friends   This'll do for tonight.
Let's go a bit further. We must keep on.
Why? Where're we going?
We should go back.
Where to? – there's nowhere anymore.
We're here – we know that. We've got each other.
Stick together. No rows.
I want a drink.
The tins are for the morning.
Want mine now.
What if we can't find any more tomorrow?
I want my tin now! Hands up who wants their drink.

Hands go up.

Drinks!

The cans are handed round from the sack. They drink.

Don't have to swallow the whole can. Save some for
tomorrow.
Too thirsty.
(*Points to the* **Man**.) One for him?
Offer him. See if he takes it.

One of them holds a can in front of the **Man**'s *face. No reaction.*

Friend   Where's Lisa?

They look round.

Friends   Lazy cow. Skived off somewhere.
Who saw her last?

No response.

Someone must've spoken to her!
Me! Asked her to help me – no, that was yesterday.
One of us must've seen her! No one? – all day?
I wanted her this morning. I couldn't find her. I thought she
was around . . .
Where's Becca?

She is not there.

Friends   They've gone off together.
Last night.
Crept off while we were asleep.
Where?
To find the cops?
The rats!
There's no cops!
Get out of carrying him.
Rats!
They're lost.
(*Calls.*) Lisa! Lisa! Becca!

No answer.

We could've wasted hours looking for them.
What if they've had an accident?
Two of them? – they'd've shouted.
Gone a whole day and we didn't notice . . .

They might turn up.
They're *gone*.

They finish the drinks.

Adam   Few cans left for the morning.

Friends   Least there's food in the gardens.
Could be contaminated.
So could the tins.
Let's go to sleep.

They settle down. Silence.

We're lost.
Like being shipwrecked in the empty fields.
Why've they knocked the houses down?
We don't know where we are. We don't know where we're
going. What we're doing.
What'll become of us? What we're here for?
Is it a joke?
What's the point? – there's no one to ask.
Sleep.

They fall into an exhausted sleep. **Adam** *lies with the sack behind the
stretcher. He sits up and looks round. Slowly the* **Man** *lifts his head and
sits up. His eyes meet* **Adam***'s. They stare at each other. The* **Man**
feebly puts out both hands as if in blessing.

Man (*half-trance*)   Bless you . . . good kids . . . bless . . .

The **Man** *sinks back onto the stretcher.* **Adam** *goes to the* **Man** *and
looks down at him. The* **Man** *sleeps.* **Adam** *looks wearily round at all
the sleepers and discarded cans. Chaos. He touches an empty can with his
toe. He goes to the sack. Stoops over it. Suddenly* **Tasha** *jumps up and
hurls herself on to* **Adam***'s back.*

Tasha   Bastard! Bastard!

Tasha *and* **Adam** *fight. The others wake.*

Friends   What? What? What's that?
Attack! Cops!
(*Sleeper trodden on.*) Ouch! Get off!

Tasha   Nicking!

Adam   Liar!

Suddenly half the friends are fighting and shouting. The others try to stop them. The **Man** *sleeps in the middle of it. He turns on his side and curls up like a baby.*

Friends   What is it?
They've come!
Get off!
Kill you!

Tasha   Nicking! Nicking!

Adam   Liar.

Tasha   Nicking! Saw you!

Adam   Let go! I'll break your neck!

Friends   Stop it! Stop it! Stop it!

The fighting stops. **Tasha** *is holding on to* **Adam**.

Friends   You tore my jacket!
You hit me first!
I never!
Did! Did!

Adam   Get off!

Friend   You started it!

Tasha   *I* started it! He was nicking cans!

Adam   Liar! Take it back!

Tasha   I saw you! (*Points to the sack.*) There!

Adam   You're mad! Say it once more – I'll break your neck!

Tasha   Thief.

Tasha *and* **Adam** *fight. The others stop them.*

Friends   Stop it! Break it up!
Let him speak.

Tasha *and* **Adam** *are parted. They shout across the sleeping* **Man**.

Tasha   Saw him! Nicking cans out the sack!
All we got left!

Adam   She accuses me again I'll kill her!

Tasha   Thief! Thief!

They restrain **Adam**. *He breaks away. They stare at him.*

Adam   I was clearing up the cans.

Friend (*sarcasm*)   Can't you think of something better than
that?

Adam   I can't stand the mess! (*He starts to gather the empty cans.*)
We're walking through a desert! Ruined houses! Everything
falling down! And we drop our litter like pigs! (*Someone is in his
way.*) Move! (*He picks up a can.*) I don't know what's happening!
Why it's falling apart! Where everyone's gone! But I'm not an
animal! (*A few of the others help him. He picks up the last can.*) It
offends me!

A **Friend** *holds the sack open.* **Adam** *puts the cans into it. He takes
the sack and starts to go.*

Tasha   Where you going?

Adam   Chuck your rubbish in the ditch! Objections?

Adam *goes out. Silence.*

Friend   Lisa and Becca should've said they were going.

Not slunk off. If anyone wants to go they can.

We're free. But we ought to say.

The **Friends** *nod and murmur agreement.*

Tasha (*looking off*)   Look at him emptying the sack in the
ditch. Going through the motions as if he meant it. I saw him!

Friend   We've got to stick together.

Silence. They settle down again. **Adam** *comes back.* He carries the
empty sack.

Tasha   Don't look at me like that!

Adam   I can look how I like.

Friends *groan.*

Tasha   You were stealing!

Adam   Say that again!

Tasha   Thief!

Tasha *and* **Adam** *fight. Suddenly they are all fighting – lashing in panic, shouting, crying.*

Friends   Kill you!
Bastard!
Kill you!
Kill you!
Kill you!

Some of them chase others off.

Come back! Come back!
Stop!

The rest go out fighting and calling. The **Man** *lies alone. He does not move. Off, calls and sounds of the fight.* **Jill** *and* **Mark** *come back.*

Mark   Bring him! We'll lose them in the dark!

Jill *throws the sack on to the stretcher.*

Mark   Quick! Take your end! Catch them up!

Jill   They're crazy!

Jill *and* **Mark** *carry out the stretcher. Off, sounds of fighting.*

Eight

Journey.
Afternoon, a week later.

Joe *and* **Jill** *come on walking ahead of the others.* **Jill** *stops.*

Jill (*points*)   Those trees are dying. I think the soil's turning grey.

They sit.

Joe   They said this would happen. It was on the news.

Jill   Not this. This is too quick.

Joe   Suppose it comes to a point where it *has* to happen. After that you can't stop it.

Jill   Perhaps we should camp here and let it happen.

Joe   Have to move on for food.

Jill   When winter comes –

Joe (*stands, calls*)   Oi! (*To* **Jill**.) We'll manage all right.

Jill   Don't believe it any more. We're going towards something terrible.

Joe   Don't scare the others.

Jill   Why did your mother make you burn the house?

Joe (*calls*)   Keep up! (*To* **Jill**.) She was confused.

Jill   She must have known the people in it.

Joe (*calls*)   You can do it! (*To* **Jill**.) Perhaps she didn't. She wasn't happy. That's why she was always trying to enjoy herself. (*Calls.*) Come on!

Jill   Hard work carrying him. D'you think it's time to . . . ?

Joe   No.

Jill   Do we have to carry him all the way?

Joe   We can't leave him.

Jill   Some of them want to. That's why they go. It gets harder for us.

Joe   Let them go. They don't say goodbye because they're ashamed. It's like walking off and leaving us at our own funeral. If we stick together we've got a chance. He's getting better. He sits up. When he can walk he can choose what he does. I think he's the only thing keeping us together. After all this, if we could walk off and leave someone to starve to death – what's the point of anything? If there was only *me* left – I still wouldn't leave him. They need a hand. (*Calls.*) Hold on. We're coming.

They go out the way they came.

Nine

Journey.
Evening, two weeks later.

Matt *and* **Georgie** *carry on the stretcher. The* **Man** *lies flat with his eyes open.*

Matt   Take a rest.

Georgie   Fifteen minutes to go.

Matt   Carried him up the hill. Counts as double.

They put down the stretcher.

Man   Good kids. Bless you.

The others have come back from the path ahead. Eleven are left. Their clothes are torn and dirty.

Friend   You stopped!

Matt   Arm ache.

Jill   Village up there. Found a tap. Had a wash.
You go up. You'll feel better.

Matt   In a minute. Breath back first.

Friend (*to* **Man**)   You can wash too.

Jill   We'll bring you a basin of water.

Joe   No let him walk.

Man   My legs.

Joe   We'll help you.

Man   They won't hold up.

Joe   You're afraid we'll leave you when you can walk. You can stay with us as long as you like. It'd be easier for us if you can walk. (*Goes to the stretcher.*) I'll help you.

Joe *pulls back the blankets and takes the* **Man**'*s hands. Helps him to stand. The* **Man** *collapses, puts his arms round* **Joe** *and clings to him.*

Man   My legs!

Joe   Try! (*To the others.*) Grab the other side.

They help the **Man** *to walk. One of them takes a piece of towel from the stretcher.*

Joe   See! – you can!

Man   No no.

Friends   Great!
Like teaching a baby to walk!

Man   Ah! Ah!

They take the **Man** *out.* **Matt** *and* **Georgie** *are left.* **Matt** *drops on to the stretcher to rest.* **Georgie** *sits with his back to it.*

Matt   My whack for today.

Georgie   It was easier when we had the others.

Matt   Don't blame them for going.

Georgie   Why do they go in pairs? Ron and Paul didn't even like each other.

Matt   Coincidence. Have you thought of it?

Georgie   What?

Matt   Do a runner. We don't have to stay. It was Joe's problem. I'm sorry I came.

Georgie (*changes the subject*)   Let's make his bed!

Give the blankets a shake! Up – lazy sod!
Grab that end!

Matt *stands. They take a piece of blanket from the stretcher. Shake it.*

Georgie   Phew – dust! We're carrying round an acre of dirt!

Matt   Do the pillow!

Georgie *picks up the pillow. Shakes it. A brick falls out.*

Georgie   A brick!

Matt   Brick? That's why he's heavy! A blinking brick!
What's he want a brick for.

Georgie   Chuck it!

The **Man** *lurches on.*

Man   Don't!

Georgie *throws the brick aside.*

Man   My things! My things!

Matt   Making your bed!

Man   Don't touch!

Georgie   Make you more comfortable!

Man   Leave it!

Matt   It's full of dust!

The **Man** *holds out both his hands as if he is about to fall forwards.*

Man   Help me.

*They catch him and help him to the stretcher. He sits on the side, fidgets
with the covers, straightens them.*

Yes yes . . . shouldn't have walked . . . the pain's worse . . .
didn't mean to shout . . . get angry. You're good kids, bless
you. (*Pats the stretcher.*) My home. Wouldn't have survived
without you.

Matt   What's the brick for?

Man   My head. A hard pillow helps the pain.

The others have come back along the path. One carries the piece of towel.

Joe   He's all right?

Friend (*towel*)   Dropped it.

The **Man** *takes the piece of towel. Tucks it under the pillow.*

Matt   Stop here for the night.

Jill   Too late to go on. We'll go up to the village tomorrow. Nick some breakfast.

They settle down. The **Man** *lies on the stretcher. Quiet.*

Matt   Should post a lookout.

Friend   No one'll bother us here.

Matt   You don't know.

Friends   Need our sleep if we're keeping this pace up. He means to keep a watch on *us*. We don't trust each other any more.

Matt   Do two-hour turns.

Friend   You go first.

Matt   All right. Who's second?

Georgie   Me.

Friend   I'll go third.

Matt   That's settled then.

They settle down and fall quiet.

Jill   We don't say good night any more.

No one responds. **Matt** *stands guard at the side, looking off. The others sleep. Silence.*

The **Man** *sits up on the stretcher. He looks round. Stands slowly. Takes the piece of towel from under the pillow. Starts to go to the brick. Stops once to look round at* **Matt** *–* **Matt** *has his back to him. He reaches the*

brick, picks it up and puts it in his pocket. He goes silently to **Matt**.
Throws the towel over **Matt**'s *head – rapid mechanical efficiency –
smothers him – brings him down. Takes the brick from his pocket – hits*
Matt *once on the head. Drags him out. He has done everything with
lethal military neatness.*

Friend (*asleep, murmuring*)   No . . . please . . .

All the sleepers begin to murmur. The **Man** *comes back. He holds the
brick in one hand, the piece of towel trails from the other. His coat is
longer and his face is whiter. He goes to the sleepers to choose the next –
walking among them, stepping over them. The murmur rises in piteous
sobs and wails. Slowly it swells into a great arc of lamentation and
tumult – echoes sounding inside echoes – torn, solemn, beautiful – the
sorrow, frustration and longing of childhood.*

The **Man** *chooses* **Tasha**. *Stoops over her.*

Tasha (*asleep, sobs*)   His shadow's falling on me in the dark.

The **Man** *turns away. The sound begins to die into stillness and peace.
The* **Man** *goes to the stretcher. Puts the brick under the pillow. Wipes
his hands on the piece of towel and neatly tucks it under the pillow. Lies
down to sleep.*

The sleepers are silent. **Georgie** *wakes. Looks round.*

Georgie (*whispers.*)   Matt . . . (*Gets up. Whispers.*)
Time to stand down.

He looks round. Goes out.

(*Off, calls in a whisper*) Matt you there? My turn.

Silence. He comes back.

He's gone! That's why he wanted to be lookout!
So he could run! (*Yells into the darkness.*) Bastard!
Bastard! You bastard!

The others are waking, getting to their feet.

Friends   What is it?
Matt's gone!
Traitor!

Don't call him names! – he must've heard something – gone
to look –

Georgie   The bastard! When you were at the tap – he tried
it on with me! Tried to talk me into it!

Naomi (*hysteria*)   No! No! Stop it! Stop it! Stop it!
You're playing with me!
You'll all run – leave me to die!

Tasha/Jill (*comforting* **Naomi**)   We won't – we won't.

Naomi   It's him! He burnt the house! Burnt the boy!
He'll kill me! Murderer! Murderer!

Naomi *runs out.*

Friends   I've had enough! I'm off too!
Stop!
You'll break your necks in the dark!
Hold on! I'm coming! It's a trap!

They all run out after **Naomi**. *The* **Man** *is alone. He does not move.*
Gemma *and* **Frank** *run in.*

Georgie (*off*)   Bring him!

Gemma *and* **Frank** *pick up the stretcher. Off,* **Naomi** *screams,*
others shout.

Gemma   Careful! Get the end!

Frank   It's all right! The walking's put him out!

Gemma *and* **Frank** *start to carry out the stretcher.*

Georgie (*off*)   Here!

Gemma *and* **Frank** *swing the stretcher round and go in the other*
direction.

Frank (*calls*)   Hold on! Wait!

Gemma *and* **Frank** *run out with the stretcher.*
Off, screams and shouts.

Ten

Journey.
Night, a week later.

The stretcher is carried on by the five survivors – **Joe**, **Jill**, **Stacey**, **Marvin**, **Donna**. *The* **Man** *lies prone.*

Marvin Stop now please.

Stacey It's dark. It scares me.

Marvin (*stops*) Can't any more.

Jill We'll leave you behind.

The others go on. They stop and look back at **Marvin**.

Marvin (*lowers his head*) Sorry.

Donna Perhaps we should split up. Try our luck on our own.

They put down the stretcher.

Stacey I'm scared of the dark. I'd grown out of that.

Donna I think the world's dying. There's no one any more. No one looks for us. No one remembers us. I feel old. It must be like this. We've grown old and don't understand it yet. Shall we split up?

The **Man** *sits up on the stretcher.*

Man (*points*) Look – dark shapes on the horizon.

They look and see nothing.

See!

Stacey No.

Man Like dark mountains. *The port*! I worked there.

They look and still see nothing. They turn to look at each other.

Man You're good children. Carried me so far. Now I can help you. Stay together. You'll reach the port in two days. The warehouses are like great cliffs – both sides of the street – they make the highways look like little alleys. They're stacked with food and clothes and videos and discs. All you want. Now everywhere's deserted it's yours. Go in and take your pick. There'll be chemists – medicines – my cure. (*Points.*) I see the dark shape with my sailor's eyes. The lights'll come on soon. It's where we've been coming all the time. In two days we'll be there. The dark port on the edge of the sea.

They look away.

Donna   Marvin?

Joe   Asleep.

Jill   We ought to eat.

Stacey   Sick of mouldy scraps. Let's get up early. Reach the port tomorrow. In a day.

They stand and stare towards the port. **Marvin** *sleeps at their feet.*

Stacey   . . . have a feast . . .

Joe   . . . a party . . .

Jill   . . . burn our rags . . . dress up . . .

They stare in silence.

Donna   Marvin's turn to be lookout.

Man   I'll do it for him. Let me.

Jill   Are you sure?

Man   It's only right I do my share. I can watch from my bed. (*Points.*) Move it there.

They move the bed to the side.

Bless you. Sleep while I watch.

Jill   Wake me, remember. It's my turn next.

They settle into exhausted, feverish sleep.

Man   If you make an early start you'll be in port tomorrow. (*He hums a few notes.*) Sea shanty. We sang ourselves to sleep at

sea . . . In port the streets were lit all night. Houses. Halls.
Dockside taverns. Music and dancing. The smell of food on
spits. (*Sings a few notes. His voice breaks.*) I caught a sickness in a
foreign port. The lungs. I couldn't speak. A strange croaking
in my throat. I left the sea. Went inland. (*Points.*) The lights are
on. We saw them from the other side – the middle of the dark
sea. The pilot took us in – past little boats bobbing like hands
drowning by the quays. Different colours. Cardigans on the
wrists. The mothers knit them.

The sleepers begin to talk.

Joe/Jill/Donna/Stacey/Marvin

. . . port . . . tomorrow . . . music . . . clothes . . . dancing . . .

*The **Man** stands. He takes the towel from under the pillow. Unwraps
the brick. Goes to **Stacey**. Kneels.*

Stacey   . . . in a day . . . in a day . . .

*The **Man** throws the towel over **Stacey**'s face – fast, mechanical,
efficient – **Stacey** stiffens – smothered – struggles – he drags her to the
stretcher – throws her on it – hits her once with the brick: she is still. He
lifts the towel from her face. Stoops to peer at her for a moment. Swings
her fully onto the stretcher. He walks among the sleepers – the brick in one
hand, the towel trailing from the other – searching as if he were lost. He
sits down in the middle of the sleepers.*

Man   When I was a sailor one day I said I'll take my son to
sea. Show him the world. The good. The bad. The violence
that destroys it. (*Looks at the sleepers.*) If it was different we'd be
friends. Take care of you. Treat you as mine. So much to
learn before we know ourselves. (*He has begun to cradle the brick
and stroke it.*) Lately my sickness has been worse. I shan't
survive. A few more days then dead. (*Hums a few notes.*) My son
my son . . . (*Stops.*) Time!

*Suddenly he twists to the side – flaring the towel – falls on **Donna** –
smothers her – kills her with a blow of the brick.*

Man   Hgn.

*Immediately he jumps up – runs to **Marvin** – drops the towel – runs* *back for it –* **Marvin** *stirs – he leaves the towel – turns to* **Marvin** *– falls on him – raises the brick – brings it down –* **Marvin** *– half-asleep – moves his head aside – the brick hits the ground: crash!*

Marvin *wakes – the brick is striking at him again – he swings his head – the brick misses – hits again – head swings – misses – hits – head swings – misses – hits: kills.*

Jill *is on her feet.* **Joe** *is kneeling. Both transfixed in a nightmare. The* **Man** *lurches towards* **Jill**.

Man   Hgn. (*He swings the brick at her.*) Hgn – !

Jill *backs. The* **Man** *doubles over – retching – frantic – sways like a hamstrung beast.*

Man (*harsh, strangled croaking*)   Hhggnnnn! – (*Still doubled – swaying – advancing – swings at* **Jill**.) Hgn! – Hgn! –

Jill *and* **Joe** *run out. The* **Man** *still doubled – swaying like a wounded beast – scything the ground with the brick.*

Man   Hgn! Hgn!

He falls on his knees and beats the ground with the brick.

Man (*Calls.*)   Feel it! Shake! The ground! My footsteps!

He gets to his feet. Looks at the bodies. Kicks at one of them.

Get them! – like you!

He mutters to himself as he drags **Donna** *and* **Marvin** *to the stretcher and throws them on it.*

No matter. No matter. (*He collapses on the bodies.*) You. In it. All of you. All pay! (*Calls.*) All! All! With your brick! Yours! I saw you at it! (*Almost inaudibly.*) No matter. No matter.

He goes to the towel. Picks it up. Stands still and straight. Wipes his face on the towel with one upwards movement of his hands. Presses it against his face.

(*Groans.*) No matter.

He takes the towel from his face. Goes to the stretcher, wrenches it round. Stops to breathe. Wheels out the stretcher.

Eleven

Port.
Morning.

Joe *comes on. He carries bags of tins, gadgets, clothes. They spill on to the ground. He is playing a radio. He can't find the music he wants. He puts the bags on the ground. Fiddles with the tuning.*

The ghost of the **Stranger** *appears. He wears the puppet's clothes and has the same hair and eyes.*

Joe   Boy from new estate. You're not real. In my head. Make you up. Did the fire hurt?

Stranger   At first. It didn't last.

Joe *(gestures to bags)*   Tins. Racks of clothes. Videos. Shopping city – empty – no one selling – music – power from the sun. Go in and take. *(Turns radio off, drops it.)* Trash.

Stranger   My father drove down the street. Saw the fire. People watching. Tried to put his key in the lock. Twisted by the heat. He kicked the door in. A great red tongue of fire roared out at him – the door was like an open mouth, the house shouting in pain. Firemen tried to stop him. Black suits. I was dead but I saw them. My father running up the stairs. They fell down as he jumped on them. His coat was burning. He reached out to grab me. I was a bundle of fire. I burnt in his arms. He dropped me. I fell down into the house. The ground was burning. It was a burning pit. I was dead, I didn't feel it. My father breathed the fire. Black smoke burnt his lungs. They took him to hospital on a stretcher. I think he couldn't forget he saw me in the fire. He left the hospital to find you.

Joe   Why don't I like the music? Or dress up? Or pig myself on grub?

Stranger   I'm glad you brought me here.

Joe   I heard you in the fire.

Stranger   I know.

Joe   I could have called the firemen sooner.

Stranger   I know.

Joe   I ran along the ditch. Tripped over the rat.

Stranger   I came to forgive you.

Joe   Forgive me?

Stranger   Yes you didn't mean to kill me –

Joe   But –

Stranger   And anyway I was dead by then. Don't forget me. I wish we could be friends. We could play your radio. Explore the port. Go to the –

The **Man** *charges on. His face is whiter, his coat is longer – it whirls round him as he runs.*

Man   The last!

The **Man** *leaps on* **Joe**. *A fight. The* **Man** *gasps for breath, breathes hoarsely. He reels from the fight.*

Joe   Your son! There!

The **Man** *looks. The ghost has gone. The* **Man** *howls in despair.*

Man   My son's dead! (*Turns to Joe and suddenly shrinks into petty, seething rage.*) Your mother was a whore. She worked for me. I kept the money. Bought the house. She wanted to move in with me. No! I moved in with my wife! Your mother wanted revenge! She burnt the house! (*Gestures.*) They only *knew* – the ones I killed. You *did* it! (*Shudders as he takes the brick from his pocket.*) *You* killed my son!

He lunges at **Joe**. **Joe** *runs out. The* **Man** *collects the dropped gear.*

(*Mutters as he picks up the pieces.*) . . . his . . . his . . . his . . .

He becomes very old and frail. His breath rattles in his throat. He drags out the bags.

Twelve

Port.
Later.

Joe *comes on. He carries nothing.*

Joe   I've got everything. I'm the last person in the world.
I must find someone.

Goes.

For Nathaniel New

Have I None

Have I None was first presented by Big Brum on 2 November 2000 at Castle Vale Artsite, Birmingham. The cast was as follows:

Sara	Amanda Finney
Jams	Richard Holmes
Grit	Bobby Colvill

Director Chris Cooper
Designer Ceri Townsend

Time
18 July 2077

Note
Have I None is the third play in the Big Brum trilogy written by Edward Bond for the Big Brum Theatre-in-Education Company, based in Birmingham. The two earlier plays are *At the Inland Sea* and *Eleven Vests*.

One

A room with a wall at the back. In it, a door leading to a street. A kitchen off to the left. A small narrow oblong table and two chairs – all matching, utilitarian, black wood. No other furniture or decoration.

Sara *sits in one of the chairs. She listens intensely.*
Silence.
A knock at the door. It is insistent but not aggressive.
Sara *does not move.*
Silence.
Sara *stands and goes to the door. She opens it. No one is there. She stands in the doorway and looks out. She turns back to the room and closes the door. She goes back to the same chair. Sits.*
Silence.
Sara *stands and goes to the door. She stops by it. Listens.*
Pause.

Sara   Go away! Go away! (*Pause.*) What d'you want? (*She bangs on the door.*) You hear!

Silence.

Sara *snatches at the handle – yanks the door open. No one is there. She closes the door and walks back into the room.*
Short pause.
A knock.
Sara *stands still.*
Pause.
Sara *goes to the table and sits in the same chair.*
Silence.
The door opens. **Jams** *comes in. He wears a simple black uniform.*

Jams   'Lo.

He kisses the side of **Sara**'s *cheek. He goes out into the kitchen.*
Sara *sits looking at the door.*

Jams (*off*)   Guess what happened on patrol.

Sara *doesn't move.*
Pause.

Jams *comes back. He has taken off his jacket and is hanging it on a wire coat hanger.*

Jams Guess what happened on patrol today. Things people get up to! We were in the old town. Part they cleared years ago. Bandits hide up there sometimes. We saw an old woman walking on the street ahead of us. Told the driver to slow down. Guess what she was carrying. You all right?

He goes out into the kitchen.

(*Off.*) Carrying it under her arm. Picture!

Sara *goes quietly to the door and opens it. As* **Jams** *talks she looks out. Then she closes it and goes back to the same chair. Sits.*

Jams (*off*)   Couldn't see what it was of. Had it hugged to her side. She kept getting lost. Stopped at the crossroads – looked round – then trotted off. She knew where she was heading. Didn't see us. Didn't look round once. The lads wanted to pick her up. I said no, wait – see what she's up to.

He comes in. He is wearing civvy trousers.

Big picture under her arm. Told the driver to close up. We were almost running her shadow down. She must've heard the engine if she wanted. She wasn't talking to herself – not loony that way. Lads were edgy. They can handle bandits. Not old ladies carrying a picture in the ruins. Uncanny. What if they're making it up in their heads? All of 'em? Possible. Mass hallucinations. Effect of ruins. Why you sitting there? We going to eat?

Jams *sits in the chair facing* **Sara**.
A knock.
Sara *looks sideways down at the table.*

Jams   She turns off on this track. Side road once. Lepal Street – sign still up. She goes through a door. Told the driver to drive past. Looked through the holes in the wall. Vanished. Stopped the truck. Went back with Dinny. Crep' in the doorway. The old biddy's inside. Picture stood on the rubble by the wall. She's grubbing about in the dirt. What's she lost?

You listening to me? (*No reaction.*) A nail! She's looking for a
nail.

Three knocks. **Sara** *does not react.*

Jams   The other lads'd left the vehicle. Gawping through
the holes. Didn't say so she'd hear: used me hands. Sent 'em
back. Leaving the vehicle unattended! – could be a trap.

A knock.

The old biddy's found a table. Dragging it over the rubble –
hard work I can tell you! – it's bucking about like a calf being
dragged to the butchers! Coat and blouse hanging undone.
Hate slovenliness! Catches her hem in her heel. Rip. What a
mess!

A knock.

Jams   The table's there – eventually. Climbs on. Bangs the
nail in the wall with a brick. Brick breaks. Scrapes the skin off
her fingers. Blood. Looks round for the picture. It's left on the
pile by the wall. I go in. Hang the picture on the wall. See her
close up. Long white eyebrows hanging in her eyes like dead
spiders. She starts to pee herself. Trickles down on the table.
Runs her hand through her hair. Leaves a red streak on the
grey. Chriss she'll stink the cab out! I'm sitting up front with
the driver! She never looked at the picture. Weren't even
straight. Sea. Forest – mountains behind. The table's like a
butcher's block: blood, piss. She's stood on the edge. Rocks –
the leg's skewing off. Can't give her a hand, can't touch
anything like that. She comes down – jumps or topples – skins
her shins. Screeches like a nail skidding down a glass runway.
Chriss I'm definitely sitting in front! – blood – piss – now
hollering! She didn't though. Just gurgles with the snot up her
snout. That dick Johannson's still in the gap. Stayed when I
sent 'em back. I beckoned him with one finger – and point
down to the bitch on the bricks. Not a dicky-bird – did it by
pointing. That narked him. He had to drag her to the vehicle.
We drove her to the centre. They won't feed her. Her age why
prolong the misery? We played football with the picture.
Kicked it under the rubble – where the CO can't see it if he

comes snooping. They cleared those houses since thirty years back. They weren't allowed to take their old stuff with them. Where's she hid a picture all them years? (*Shrugs.*) Probably weren't hers. Found it on a dump. Not her house. All look the same when they're knocked down. Not even her street. Could've been a – (*Violently smashes a fist on the table.*) What did I say?

Sara   I –

Jams   What? What? Tell me!

Sara   I –

Jams   You're not listening!

Sara   Picture – a woman –

Jams (*bangs both fists on the table*)   And? – And? – You're not listening!

Jams *gets up and walks away.*

Sara   I've got – I want to tell you about –

Jams   I come home! Try to be sociable! Interest you in my work! (*Goes to the table. Bangs it.*) You can't even listen! Sit there! Nothing to eat!

Sara   I – (*Stops.*)

Jams   I? – I?

Sara   Please listen. Someone knocks on the door.

Jams   What? (*Looks at the door.*) I didn't hear it.

Sara   They knock all the time.

Jams *goes to the door. Opens it. No one is there. He shuts the door and turns back to* **Sara**.

Jams   What's going on?

Sara   It keeps knocking all day.

Jams   Kids.

Sara   I'd've heard them laugh or run away.

Jams   How long's it been going on?

Sara   Weeks. I can't imagine it!

Jams (*slight pause*)   Let me get this right. You hear a knock –
open the door – no one's there?

Sara   Yes.

Jams   You're going potty.

He goes into the kitchen. **Sara** *sits in silence.* **Jams** *comes back. He is
taking his jacket off the hanger.*

Weeks? Why didn't you tell me? The service expects us to
keep to standards! Be respectable! Not get involved in this
shite! There's enough shite outside! It's not coming in my
house! (*He throws the coat hanger on the floor. He gets into his jacket.*)
I'll eat at the canteen! Pick that up!

Jams *goes out. He shuts the door behind him.* **Sara** *picks up the coat
hanger. She stands in the room and stares at the door. Silence. She goes out
into the kitchen.*

Two

The room is empty.
A knock at the door.
Pause.
A knock at the door.
Jams *comes in from the kitchen. He wears civvies. He forks food from a
plate he holds in his hand. He opens the door.* **Grit** *stands there. He
wears an old fawn mack and a battered brown trilby. He has a backpack
on his back.*

Grit   Hello. I got your number down the street. Is your wife
in? – you must be her husband: they said she was – (*He stops.*)

Jams *watches* **Grit**. *He puts a forkful of food in his mouth.*

Jams   What you want her for?

Grit   Is she in?

Jams   Might be.

Grit   O it's nothing private. It's just – better if I tell her. Or you both together. Will she be long? I'll come back.

Jams *steps aside and motions* **Grit** *in with his fork.* **Grit** *comes in.* **Jams** *pushes the door to with his foot. He chews and watches* **Grit**.

Jams   She's out.

Grit   Just take this off. Heavy.

He takes off the backpack and puts it on the floor. **Jams** *forks food into his mouth.*

Grit   . . . If I'm interrupting I'll come back in . . .

Jams   What you want her for?

Grit   I'm her brother.

Jams   Are you?

Grit   I live – I lived – at the other end of the country. (*Gestures to pack.*) Walked down.

Jams   Walked?

Grit   No travel document.

Jams   Why?

Grit   Office wasn't functioning. Official came out and told the queue no more documents issued. The staff were throwing themselves off the roof. Couldn't use transport without a document.

Jams (*wags fork at* **Grit**)   You've got a suicide outbreak.

Grit   Nothing worked. No jobs. No electricity. Water comes out with lumps. On the way to work I had to cross a bridge. Crowd on it. Sitting and standing both sides on the parapets. Done up in overcoats. Looked like rows of pigeons – roosting or walking up and down looking for a place. Then one of them'd throw theirself in the river. That started it. Splash – splash – splash. Five or six throw themselves in. Others climb up to fill the gaps they left. The ones in the river float off.

Their overcoats are blown out on top of the water like bladders or big blisters. When I got to work it had reached there – it was closed.

Jams (*sits at the table and eats*)   The faces are the give-away. They all jumped? No one used a rope or anything fancy?

Grit   No.

Jams   They all do the same – whatever it is. One of the symptoms. Know Reading?

Grit   No.

Jams   Place down this end. Suburb before it was resettled. They had an outbreak. I was sent because of the job. They walked the streets carrying a knife in front of them – like this. (*He holds his fork at arm's length.*) Point up. Hundreds of 'em. Streets were chocker. Going up and down. Like sleepwalkers holding a candle out. Dead quiet. No one spoke. No one bumped into anyone. All of a sudden one of 'em'd stab theirself. Stab stab stab. Hacking and ripping. Arms and legs. Chest. Neck. As if they wanted to stab themselves as many times as they could before the knife fell out of their hand. Never stabbed anyone else. Rest didn't turn round. Saw one on the pavement. Trying to reach the knife he'd dropped. Scrabbled round for it for half an hour. When he got it all he could do was scratch the pavement. Rest step over him. They all wore scarves – like yours wore overcoats. The symptoms are always the same. That's why I asked if you saw their faces. Blanks.

Grit   Yes.

Jams   If you'd been resettled it wouldn't've happened. Reading wasn't resettled either. No outbreaks after.

He stands and takes the plate and towel into the kitchen. **Grit** *unfastens the backpack. He takes out an envelope and puts it in his inside pocket. He fastens the backpack.* **Jams** *comes from the kitchen drying the plate on a tea towel.*

Jams   You haven't been hanging round outside playing silly buggers with door knockers?

Grit No.

Jams If you have I'll find out. (*No response.*) A long way to come. Why?

Grit When I got home my wife was gone. Didn't know if she'd killed herself. Could've been on the bridge when I crossed. Searched to see if she'd left a note. Didn't take long. Up there it's like here, by the looks of it: authority discourages furniture. I tried the drawer of our table. Never normally touch it, that was her responsibility. It was stuck. I yanked it out. The runner was loose. She'd propped it up with a bit of card. When I unrolled it it was a photo.

Jams Not allowed. All personal papers destroyed when they abolished the past.

Grit This got lost in the drawer.

A sound at the door.

Jams Her. Tidy this up.

Jams *takes the plate and tea towel out into the kitchen. The door opens.* **Sara** *comes in carrying in front of her an issue box of food. She closes the door with her heel. She looks over the box at* **Grit**.

Grit He let me in.

Sara *goes towards the kitchen.*

Sara (*calls*) You there?

She turns to look at **Grit**. **Jams** *comes from the kitchen.*

Jams I'll take it. (*He takes the box.*) He says he's from the other end.

He takes the box out into the kitchen.

(*Off.*) Walked. Your brother.

Sara (*calls*) What?

Jams (*off*) Brother.

Grit You don't remember me.

Sara   I haven't got a brother. No one has. They did away with all that. What d'you want? (*Calls.*) Why did you let him in? – You can't walk in a house and say you're a brother. What are you after?

Jams *comes from the kitchen.*

Jams   You still haven't said what you've come for.

Sara   I don't care what he's come for! Get rid of him!

Grit *takes the envelope from his inside pocket. He takes a photo from the envelope. He holds it out to* **Sara**.

Grit   Look.

Sara   What is it?

Grit   Photo. (*To* **Jams**.) From the drawer. (*To* **Sara**.) You years ago.

Sara *stares at* **Grit** *and then turns to* **Jams**. *No one moves.*

Grit   I came to deliver it.

He puts the photo on the table.

I'd forgotten you. Couldn't have said your name if I had to. When I saw the photo – as I unrolled it – my mouth said it – out loud. It knew, I didn't. I said 'What?' It said it again: Sally.

Jams *goes to the table and picks up the photo. He looks at it. Tears it up.*

Jams   She's Sara. Could be any two kids.

Sara   What's he want?

Jams (*shrugs*)   Suicide outbreak up there.

Sara   He doesn't know what he's doing! When there's an outbreak of suicide everyone imagines! Hallucinates! If he *was* my brother – that's a reason to get rid of him! (*Straightens a chair.*) Some of the packs were frozen. They have to go in the fridge. (*Turns to* **Grit**.) Don't stand there! Go away!

Grit   Perhaps I was wrong when I said your name. It might've been shock because it was a photo – *any* photo. But when I was walking I remembered other things. You do when you start. When that photo was taken you said your dress wasn't right. You went out to change it. I remember watching the door. You came back with a red ribbon in your hair. You made me wipe my shoes. You said when we looked at the photo years later we'd want it to be right. I was cross. You said smile. The camera was on a chair. You set the timer. Ran back and stood by me. It whirred and clicked. I remember it.

Jams   They won't let you stay. No right to come without the document.

Grit   They weren't being issued.

Jams   If you didn't want to throw yourself off like the rest, you should've stayed to help with the mess. Not wander about.

Grit   Not going yet. Tired. Rest. Go in the morning.

He sits at the table and rests his head on his arms.

When they jumped they were like shadows falling into the water.

He sleeps. **Jams** *and* **Sara** *stare at him.*

Jams   He sat on the chair.

Sara   You let him in.

Jams   He's your brother!

Sara   He's not my brother!

Jams   He can see it's not his chair!

Sara   He might've thought it was anyone's chair!

Jams   Anyone's chair? – in somebody's house!

Sara   Visitors! Visitors! Visitors have chairs!

They are screaming.

Jams   I didn't know he'd sit in it!

Sara   You could've put names on the chairs!

Jams   Put names!

Sara   Then people would know not to sit on –

Jams   Why didn't you do it?

Sara   It's not my job!

Jams   It's not my job!

Sara   You're in the service! You're trained for emergencies!
Anyone could walk in that door and sit on –

Grit *wakes.*

Grit   Is anything wrong?

Jams/Sara   You sat in the chair!

Silence.

Jams   Who?

Sara   Who?

Jams   Who!

Sara   What who?

Jams   You said anyone could walk in that door! Who?

Sara   Who?

Jams   Who!

Sara   That's the point! *Anyone!*

Jams   Who's anyone?

Sara   God give me patience! *Anyone!*

Jams (*to* **Grit**)   Why did you sit in the chair?

Sara (*to* **Grit**, *pointing at the chairs*)   His! Mine!
(*To* **Jams**.) Yours! Mine!

Jams   I know whose chair's whose!

Sara   Sometimes!

Jams   Sometimes?

Sara Sometimes!

Jams Sometimes? What's that supposed to mean?

Sara Sometimes! I know what it means!

Jams Sometimes?

Grit I think she means sometimes it's –

Jams Shut up! I know what she means before she does!

Grit Then why did you ask her what –

Jams Shut up! Shut up!

Sara Sometimes! I keep a diary!

Jams That bloody diary!

Sara To prove what goes on! In this house you need a record! I know what happened on Friday the 22nd of June last year!

Jams Friday the 22nd of June?

Sara Friday the 22nd of June! And I know the time –

Jams Friday the 22nd of –

Sara You sat on –

Jams Liar!

Sara You sat on –

Jams Never!

Sara May I drop dead! You sat on *my* chair!

Jams (*to* **Grit**) Get out! Get out that chair!

Grit *stands.* **Jams** *leans on the chair.*

Jams Leant! Like this! (*Goes to* **Sara**.) That's what normal people call leant! Where was my backside? Not on the –

Grit *has sat in the chair.* **Jams** *turns to him.*

Jams (*to* **Grit**) To your mind is that leant? (*He notices that*

Grit *is in the chair.*) Get out of the chair! Get out!

Grit *stands.* **Jams** *leans on the chair.*

Sara   Get off my chair!

Jams   Where's my backside? Not on the seat! No way! It doesn't constitute sitting if your backside's in the air – !

Sara   No because you heard me coming and –

Jams   You don't like it when you're shown the truth!

Sara   *– got up!*

Grit *sits in the other chair.*

Jams   Did you say – did you stand in the doorway and say – when you had every opportunity – be honest for once! – did you say: you're sitting in my chair?

Sara   No!

Jams   No you did not!

They are screaming and in tears.

Sara   No! And you know why?

Jams   Tell me!

Sara   Shall I tell you?

Jams   Tell me! Tell me! I asked you!

Sara   I'll tell you why! For the same reason I keep quiet about all that goes on in this house!

Jams   You couldn't keep quiet if you were dead!

Sara *and* **Jams** *notice that* **Grit** *is sitting on the other chair.*

Sara/Jams   Get out of that chair!

Grit *stands, picks up his pack and the pieces of photo. He puts the pack on the floor, sits on the pack and methodically tries to piece back the photo.*

Sara   I know you'd been sitting!

Jams   Leant!

Sara   I can prove it!

Jams   Leant!

Sara   I heard the leg scrape! It scraped when you got out of it! I know when a leg scrapes and when it doesn't!

Jams   And I know when water runs from a tap!

Sara   I knew we'd come to that!

Jams   Water –

Sara   Tap – tap – tap – tap – tap!

Jams   – is a public resource!

Sara   One little slip! I left a tap on! You'd think I'd left Niagara Falls running in the bathroom!

Grit (*fiddling with the photo*)   All this because I sat in a chair.

Jams   *Two* chairs!

Sara   Now start on him!

Jams   You never hang your clothes up!

Sara   You take the hangers!

Jams   Of course I take the hangers!

Sara   I've never known anyone as selfish as you with hangers!

Jams   If I didn't take them they'd lie idle gathering dust!

Sara   The whole street knows what I go through if you can't get your hands on a hanger the moment you come in!

Jams   O God I pity anyone who brings a wound in this house. It'd never heal. You'd open it every night.

Sara   Wounds? I live under surveillance.

Jams   When do I ever say you –

Sara   O you don't say. You're far too clever to say. Not saying is your speciality! You're so innocent if you went paddling the sea would curdle!

Jams   What's that mean?

Silence.

Sara   I know when a chair scrapes.

Jams   And for another for-instance the time you left your shoes in the middle of the –

Sara   Tap – tap – tap – tap – tap.

Silence. **Jams** *gets up and goes to* **Grit**.

Jams   Get up! (**Grit** *looks at him.*) Up!

He jerks **Grit** *up by the collar. He throws the backpack aside and points at the spot where it was.*

There! That's not the middle of the room! That's outer space!

Sara   I'm not stupid! That's the middle of the room! It's where you kicked my shoes!

Jams   I did not kick your shoes! You put – !

Sara   Pardon me – it's in the diary – 14th September –

Jams   Tripped!

Sara   Kicked!

Jams   Tripped!

Sara   I left my shoes by the door because the 14th was wet (the meteorological office'll confirm it) and I didn't want –

Jams   Put – the middle of the room –

Sara   – to tread wet on the –

Jams   – where anyone could trip and –

Sara   – floor!

Jams   – break their neck!

Sara *slams the backpack down by the door.*

Sara   There! – that's where my shoes were left!

Grit   My pack –

Jams   Wrong! Wrong! Wrong!

Grit   Give me my –

Jams   They'd be crushed when the door's opened!

Sara   Right. Other side.

Grit *is going to pick up the backpack.* **Sara** *moves it to the other side of the door.*

Sara   I admit it. I'm not pedantic. I say when I'm wrong! The point is –

Jams *throws the backpack into the middle of the room.*

Jams   The point is *there*!

Grit *picks up the pack.*

Jams   Leave it!

Sara   Put it back!

Jams *and* **Grit** *struggle for the backpack.*

Grit   Let go!

Jams   Let go!

Sara   See what he's like! Grab grab – !

Grit   Give me my – !

Jams *gets the pack from* **Grit**. **Grit** *goes to the table, picks up a chair and puts it by the door where the backpack was.*

Sara   O my God.

Jams   O my God.

Sara   O my God.

Jams   He's ruining the home!

Grit   Now kick the chair!

Jams *sits on the chair by the door. He puts his head in his hands and groans.*

Jams   . . . It's terrible . . .

Grit   He's not kicking my pack around!

Jams (*flaring up*)   I didn't kick it!

Grit   You would next! I know what was coming!

Jams *cries.*

Sara   Don't feel sorry for him. He puts it on to get sympathy!

Grit   All this because I sat in a chair!

Jams   *Two* chairs!

Sara *turns her chair round with its back to the table.*

Sara   In future my chair faces this way! I'll eat from a tray on my lap!

Jams *gets up and turns* **Sara**'*s chair to face the table.*

Sara (*turns the chair round*)   Leave it!

Jams (*turns the chair round*)   I'll have a bit of discipline!

Grit (*examining the backpack*)   He broke the snap!

Sara (*turns the chair round*)   Freedom!

Grit (*holds out the backpack*)   Look!

Jams (*turns the chair back*)   Discipline!

Grit *picks up the other chair.*

Sara/Jams   O my God.

Grit   You're not getting this till I get a new pack! And my photo repaired!

Sara   If you hadn't let him – encouraged him – to put the photo on the table this wouldn't have –

Jams   Leave the table out of it! You're not having the table!

Jams *grabs the table, takes it to the side and hugs it.* **Sara** *picks up her chair and hugs it.* **Grit** *hugs the other chair. They stare at each other. Silence.* **Grit** *sees the backpack on the floor, rushes to it, picks it up and returns to his place. He hugs the chair and the backpack.*

Silence.

Sara *cries bitterly. She sets her chair down and sits on it.*

Sara (*crying*)   Scraped.

Sara *howls.* **Jams** *takes the chair back to its place. He fusses and adjusts its position by millimetres.* **Grit** *fiddles with the catch on the backpack.*

Grit (*fiddling*)   When they went under their breath came back in bubbles. (*The catch.*) Broke. – Your last breath in a bubble. Funny your last words floating in a bubble on the water.

Sara (*weeping bitterly*)   Scraped. It could've been the lid sliding on my coffin.

Sara *howls in despair. She gets up and takes the chair to the door.* **Jams** *adjusts the table.* **Sara** *opens the door.* **Jams** *looks up and sees* **Sara** *go through the door with the chair.*

Jams   Bring it back!

Jams *reaches – lurches – sprawls on the table and sends it flying. Crash.*

Jams   Sod it! Crucified on a table!

Grit   If the fabric wasn't fortified it've torn.

Jams *gets up and goes through the door. Pause. Off,* **Sara** *screams. Pause.* **Jams** *comes back with the chair.*

Jams   Not having her parade in the streets with a chair! If she wants to do that sort of thing she can live abroad. Shaming me to the neighbours! (*He sees* **Grit** *hugging the other chair and the backpack. He points to the table.*) There! – or I'll fold you up and put you inside your backpack!

Grit *takes the chair to the table.* **Jams** *fiddles to get the table and chairs into their exact places.* **Sara** *comes through the door with a wooden crate. She sets it against the wall.*

Sara (*to* **Grit**)   Sit.

Grit   Sit on my backpack – I sit on *that* he'll say it's his!

Sara   Sit!

Grit *picks up the crate and examines it.*

Grit   Full of splinters!

Sara   Sit!

Grit *sits on the crate. He hugs the backpack to his chest.* **Sara** *and* **Jams** *sit in the chairs at the table.*

Silence.

Jams (*to* **Grit**)   Go and use the toilet.

Grit   I don't want to use the toilet.

Jams   Use the toilet! Not having you wet the floor! That'll be next. Come down from the other end. Walk. No documentation. Sit on the chairs. *Two.* Wet the floor. There's no end to it.

Grit *stands.*

Jams (*points to the kitchen*)   There.

Grit *goes out with the backpack. Pause. A leg falls off the table.* **Jams** *stares at it.*

Jams   We'll have to kill him. He'd get out of a settlement. Look how he walked here. There's no stopping him. I can't see the future anymore, what's in it for us. Sometimes your shoelace is undone, you can't bother to stoop to tie it . . . it's easier to end it. I saw a warning at Reading. In broad daylight. People walking the streets holding a knife before them – as if they were holding a candle. He stands there breathing quietly – his breath's like a storm blowing the roof off the house.

Sara   We'll give him poison. That's convenient. We'll use the best stuff. It's like thick water. You wouldn't know it's in the spoon if the light didn't shine on it. We'll invite him to a meal to celebrate the reunion. Put it in his food. I'll go to the chemist.

Jams   Fetch my jacket. It's on the hanger.

Sara *goes out.* **Jams** *repairs the table.* **Sara** *comes back with* **Jams**'s *jacket on a hanger.* **Jams** *takes a wallet from an inside pocket. He takes a plastic card from the wallet and gives it to* **Sara**.

Jams   Put it on my card.

Jams *puts the wallet back in the jacket pocket.* **Sara** *goes out through the door. She closes it behind her.* **Jams** *works at the table a moment longer. He stands back – adjusts the place of a chair. He picks up the jacket on the hanger. He goes out to the kitchen.*

Three

The room is empty. The table, chairs and crate are in their proper places.

Grit *comes in from the kitchen. He wears his mack and trilby. He is tired and tense. He stands in the middle of the room.*
Pause.
A knock at the door.
Grit *does not move.*
Pause.
Grit *goes to the crate and sits.*
Silence.
A knock.
Grit *does not move.*
A knock.
Silence.
A knock.
Grit *stands. He goes to the door and opens it. No one is there. He goes back to the crate. He sits. He realises the door is still open. He stares at it. Pause.*
He gets up and goes to the door. He shuts it. He is halfway back to the crate.

A knock.
Grit *dashes to the door. Yanks it open. No one is there. He closes the door. He walks into the room. He hesitates.*
Silence.
The door opens quietly. **Sara** *comes in. She wears a ground-length loose coat of stiff sky-blue silk. It is covered with metal spoons. They are stitched to the silk so they cannot swing loosely but can knock against each other when the coat moves.*

Grit Where have you been? He wouldn't let me look for you. He said the service mustn't know I'm here. No one's seen you on the streets. Four days! He's out looking for you now.

Sara We played in the house when we were children. That was before they blocked the windows. I couldn't reach up to see out of them. Once you were ill. Our parents were worried. It made them hard. As if they'd been cut out of tin. The doctor wore a long black coat. I never saw his front. I thought he had two backs. *That* made him a doctor.

Grit Where did you get your coat? There are no carnivals now.

Sara In the night I came to the room where they put you. You were in a coma. I held my hand over your head. I felt the ice. There were drops all over your face. I thought that was fever: your skin cried. I knew the doctor with two backs would kill you. So I pulled back the blanket – you smelt like a stable on a frosty night – and dragged you to the window so you could see. I had to climb on a chair. Pulled you up by the shoulders. Turned your head to the window. There was nothing to see. No lights in the street. It was dark. The glass was black. I saw your face in it. It was white. Your face was talking to you. I couldn't hear it. You put out your hand. You tapped the glass. I thought you'd broken it – that was the power of fever. I nearly dropped you in fright. You'd fall on the glass. The splinters would tear off your face. The spikes would stab out your eyes. The glass wasn't cracked. What I saw was the pain in your face: your face had splintered. Your face in the glass had told you: you're dead. You slithered out of my hands. Mother ran in. I said I'd heard you moving –

found you under the window. They said yes that's the delirium. All next day I was terrified they'd find out you were dead. Blame me! – I'd dragged you. I was frightened in the way only a child can be . . . No one found out. The doctor didn't notice you were dead.

Grit   Can I sleep now you're here? I walked for months. All that time I didn't have five hours of rest. I slept like a dog – with an eye open.

Grit *lies on the floor.*

Sara   Put this under your head.

Sara *puts the backpack under his head for a pillow.*

Grit   You are my sister. I remember my face in the window.

Grit *sleeps. Slowly* **Sara** *takes off the coat, turns it inside out and puts it on again. The inside is black and covered with bones. Each bone is sewn at one end so that it hangs loose and rattles as the coat moves.*

Jams *comes through the door. He closes it behind him. He sees* **Grit** *on the floor. He kicks him.*

Jams   Up! (*He kicks* **Grit** *again.*) Up – you rubbish dump!

Grit (*stirs in his sleep*)   . . . wha'? . . .

Jams   Chriss – another burden. (*Calls to the kitchen.*) Hello! (*Waits a moment.*) No sign of her. No one's seen her. We lifted the manhole covers. Shouted down . . . I had to tell the service something. If her body had turned up and hadn't been reported absent – I'd be censured. If I can't find her or tell a good story: chop.

Sara *has sat on the crate.* **Jams** *notices that* **Grit** *is still asleep. He looks round, stares at the chairs. He puts his hands under* **Grit** *'s armpits and drags him to the table. He sits upright in a chair.* **Grit** *sleeps –* **Jams** *watches him in silence for a moment.*

Jams   I asked you to watch – for a little while. No you slept. How can I know if the service came and searched while I was out?

Jams *goes out to the kitchen. He comes back with a rope. He ties* **Grit** *to the chair. He sits at the other end of the table and watches him.* **Sara** *stands. She goes out through the door and shuts it behind her.* **Jams** *rams the table into* **Grit** *'s stomach.* **Grit** *jerks awake.*

Grit   Untie me.

Jams   Authority was right to abolish the past. Get shot of it. Videos – tapes – discos – dressing up – raves – dot com dot – junk. People were sick with it. It was a hobby to buy a new car, drive away from the salesroom and crash it into a wall. What do people do when they've got everything? One day they beg you to take it away. They want peace instead. That's why they grab at resettlement – why it's easy to forget. Everyone with the same walls – same issue furniture – same issue clothes – same issue food. It takes time – but we must. I saw the faces at Reading and pitied them. Your photo's an instance. If it had been destroyed my wife wouldn't be lost – you wouldn't be tied in the chair – I wouldn't be chopped. The suffering will end. There's still the odd lunatic. The old women with pictures in their heads. The stray kids. *I'm* not immune to it – some days I feel like the footprint in the land where no man has trod. But still it gets less. The suffering goes.

Grit   Untie me.

Jams   I'm not being chopped for you.

Grit   I won't be a bother.

Jams   No I must see this through.

Grit   I'll go far away.

Jams   No. A labour-gang was digging foundations for a new settlement. They dug into an old plague pit. They had to wear masks. There might've still been bacilli in the pit. You're a ghost in this house. A sick ghost with a disease.

The door opens. **Sara** *comes in. She wears her ordinary clothes and carries a small packet.*

Jams   Where've you been?

Sara   Lost.

Jams   For four days?

Sara   I couldn't find the way out of the ruins.

Jams   The ruins?

Sara   I wanted to see them for myself.

Jams   You were told not to go there!

Sara   I wanted to see.

Jams   For four days? I don't believe you.

Sara *sits on the crate.*

Sara   Sorry. It was like walking on a path inside a whirlwind. Round in a circle. The smaller it got the more space there was.

Jams   We sent out patrols! I made a service report!

Sara   There are so many bricks. Broken walls. Why are bricks red? I saw the tyre marks made by the trucks. I saw the footprints of people who'd lived there. They were in the houses. Turning to stone in the dust. Even the footprints of mice who'd stolen their scraps. They were in the cupboards. They'd been there for sixty generations of mice. But the generations weren't born. They were fumigated away. The time in the cupboards is mice generation 'o'.

Jams   What happened to you?

Sara   Why is he tied up?

Jams   To stop him getting lost.

Pause. **Sara** *stands and goes to the door.*

Jams   Where are you going?

Sara   I want to go to –

Jams   No! – You stay!

Silence.

Sara (*sharp*)   Why is he tied in my chair?

Jams   To stop him getting –

Sara   Why didn't you tie him in your chair?

Jams   He wasn't sitting in my chair!

Sara   You could have moved him to your chair!

Jams   I wouldn't have had to tie him in any chair if you –

Sara   Always an excuse!

Jams   Excuse?

Sara   Excuse!

Jams   It's you who needs an excuse! Four days in the –

Grit   Could you loosen this knot?

Sara   I know why you tied him in my chair!

Jams   This'll be brilliant! She had four days to work on it!

Grit   It's stopping the blood.

Sara   So he couldn't get out of it!

Jams   So he couldn't get – ! I don't believe it! Did I hear right? (*To* **Grit**.) Did you hear her say so he couldn't get out of it?

Grit   You needn't undo it – just loosen the – so I –

Sara   Yes so he couldn't get out of it.

Jams   She said it again! (*Howls with laughter. Pounds the table in hysterics.*) So he – ! (*Slaps his thighs.*) So he couldn't get out of it!

Sara   Yes and you know why?

Jams   Tell me! Tell me! So he couldn't –

Sara   I know why!

Jams   Yes?

Sara   Yes!

Jams   Tell me!

Sara   I'll tell you when I'm ready!

Jams   So he couldn't get out of it!

Sara   So he couldn't get out of it – and get into *your* chair.

Jams   Now I've heard everything!

Sara (*to* **Grit**)   Didn't he tell you to sit in my chair?

Grit   I woke up in it –

Sara   Woke up in it! Chriss I've got two bloody lunatics in the house!

Jams   That's right insult your brother!

Sara   He's not my brother!

Grit (*struggling*)   If you could slack it – the blood could –

Sara   O I know your diabolical mind! He tied you up so when I came through the door I'd be confronted with you in my chair having a sleep!

Jams   I didn't know you'd come through that door – ever!

Sara   Hoped!

Jams   Hoped?

Grit   My nose itches –

Sara   You don't get rid of me so easy! I've got my rights –

Jams   Then why did you run off to –

Sara   I wish I'd never come back –

Grit   Could you scratch it for me?

Jams   All the thanks I get! I had the manhole covers up! I was worried to –

Sara   Worried you'd lose your job!

Grit (*bends his head to the side*)   It's this side – just by the nostril –

Jams Next time don't try to come back –

Grit O dear.

Jams (*to* **Grit**) What is it mate? You got a problem?

Grit My nose –

Jams How can I help?

Grit – itches!

Jams (*to* **Sara**) – the door'll be locked!

Sara That's your idea of humanity.

Jams (*scratching* **Grit**'s *nose*) Don't teach me about humanity!

Grit Ow!

Jams Shut up!

Grit Ouch!

Jams Shut up! (*To* **Sara**.) I know how to treat my fellow man!

Grit Ow!

Sara Yes – scratching his eyes out!

Grit Ah! Other side!

Jams What?

Sara Other side!

Jams (*to* **Grit**) Why didn't you say –

Grit I couldn't get a word in edgeways!

Jams Point! You could've pointed!

Grit I can't! You tied me up!

Sara He scratched the wrong side on purpose! Tied him up – tortured him –

Jams At least I never sat on his crate!

Sara   His crate?

Jams   His crate!

Sara   Whose crate?

Grit   I don't mind who sits on my crate –

Sara (*to* **Grit**)   Your crate! You thieving little – !

Jams   Now start on your brother!

Sara   He's not my brother!

Jams   She sat on his crate while the poor lad's tied up and –

Grit   I thought you gave me the crate so I –

Sara   Shut up!

Grit   I give it back to you. Take it!

Jams (*to* **Grit**)   Shut up! (*To* **Sara**.) You gave him the crate – now you're going to steal it –

Sara   I know the sound a chair makes when it's scraped!

Jams   The shoes were in the middle of –

Sara   Tap – tap – tap – tap – tap.

Silence.

Grit   The other side itches.

Silence.

Sara   Scraped.

Silence.

Jams   I could walk in the dark. Trip. Break my neck.

Silence.

Grit *sneezes.*

Silence.

Jams   You went to the chemist?

Sara Yes.

Jams That the packet?

Sara ˙Yes.

Jams It's gift-wrapped.

Sara To avoid suspicion. He values my custom.

Jams *takes the packet out to the kitchen.*

Grit Untie me.

Sara There'd be a row. He has to do it.

Grit Were you lost?

Sara An old woman hung a picture in the ruins. I came to her place. Ended up there. Not really chance. I was looking. Saw the street sign. Hung down crooked. Lepal Street. I found the picture – its leftovers in the rubble. Splinters of wood and shreds of paper. He said it was the sea. I hammered a nail in. Hung it back on the wall. Sat there for a time. Then the top of the wall lurched sideways. Where I'd hammered the nail. Hung there for ages. Then it all came down in a rush. The bricks fell on the ground like teeth. I rested and stayed there three days. The old woman's dead. I've never seen the sea. Did you see it on your way down?

Grit No.

Sara It's shrunk. Only puddles are left. Where the sea was the sand moves as if it's still there. They say the sea's ghost walks on the shore.

Jams *comes from the kitchen with three spoons. He lays them at three places on the table.*

Jams Couple of minutes. Used dehydrated.

He goes out into the kitchen.

Grit You remember when I was ill? You came in my room one night. Sat me up in bed to make me better. You told me stories.

Sara   No. It's all in your head. I've never seen you before.

Jams *comes from the kitchen with two bowls of soup.*

Jams (*puts a bowl at one end of the table. To* **Sara**)   That's yours. (*Puts the other bowl in front of* **Grit**.) And that's yours. Bon appétit as the Germans say.

Grit   Untie me now.

Jams   When we're ready.

Jams *goes out to the kitchen.* **Sara** *goes to the table. She picks up* **Grit**'s *bowl and spoon. She stands in front of him. She dips the spoon in the soup and raises it to her lips. She breathes on it.*

Grit   I don't mind if it's hot. I'm hungry.

Sara *drinks the spoonful of soup.*

Grit (*quietly*)   . . . you bitch . . .

Sara (*calls*)   Bring some bread.

Jams (*off*)   Is none. Didn't go to the issue when you were on the run.

Sara *fills the spoon with soup.*

Grit   . . . you bitch . . .

Sara *drinks the spoonful of soup.*

Sara (*calls*)   The freezer. Thaw it in the micro.

Sara *fills the spoon with soup.*

Grit   . . . you . . . bitch . . .

Sara *is about to drink the spoonful of soup.*

Jams (*off*)   Brown or white?

Sara (*calls*)   You choose.

Sara *is about to drink the spoonful of soup.*

Jams (*off*)   Don't mind.

Sara (*calls*)   Brown.

Jams (*off*)   That does you more good.

Sara *drinks the spoonful of soup.*

Grit   If you gave me it now I'd spit it in your face.

Sara *drinks spoonfuls of soup.* **Jams** *comes from the kitchen with bread-knife, board and salt.*

Jams (*to* **Sara**)   I forgot the salt.

Jams *puts the bread-knife, board and salt on the table. Suddenly* **Grit** *thrashes in his ropes.*

Grit   Bitch! Bitch! Bitch!

Jams   The effect's almost instantaneous! (*To* **Sara**.) You got the right stuff!

Grit   She drank my soup!

Jams   What? (*He looks at the table. Points to the bowl in* **Sara***'s hands.*) No – that's his –

Grit (*struggling in the ropes*)   I hope it chokes the bitch!

Jams (*pointing*)   His! – poisoned.

Sara *cleans the inside of the bowl with her finger and licks it.*

Jams   You drank his deliberately!

Sara *drops the bowl.*

Grit   Poisoned?

Sara   Take me outside. I don't want to die in the house.

Grit   You tried to poison me!

Jams (*to* **Sara**)   Deliberately! Why? Chriss how can I explain this to the CO? The mess! What d'you want me to do!

Sara   I want to die outside – not shut in – help me.

Jams *and* **Grit** *stare at her. Suddenly* **Jams** *goes to the door and throws it open.*

Jams   Go! Get out! Get out! Get out of my house!

Sara (*bent on the table*)   I can't – get there on my – you don't need to take me far to – leave me at the corner –

Jams   Be seen in the street walking a dying woman on my arm? I won't! I can't! It's conduct unbecoming! I'd be court-martialled! Chopped! And she's my wife!

Sara *starts to sway across the room.*

Sara   . . . they'll just have to see me staggering to the . . .

Jams *goes to the table, snatches the bread-knife and slashes* **Grit** *free.*

Grit *doesn't move. He stares at* **Sara**.

Jams   Help her! She'll be dead before you've – ! You're free! Take her out! Scratch your nose! (*Stops.*) O my God it's a joke! *That's* the poison! You swapped them.

Jams *grabs the bowl and tries to poke spoonfuls of soup into* **Grit**.

Jams (*to* **Grit**) Drink it! Drink it!

Grit *stares at* **Sara**. *She crashes onto the crate.*

Sara   Help me. Don't make me stay – and have time to be sorry. Take me out. It's quicker if I walk – there won't be time to be sorry. (*Confused laughter.*) At Reading – in the street – in broad daylight – they carried daggers before them – as if they were –

Grit *stands. He helps* **Sara** *to her feet.*

Grit   Why? Why did you do it?

Sara   Don't talk . . . Outside . . . talk to me there . . .

Jams (*watching* **Grit** *help* **Sara** *to the door*)   O my God. O my God. O my God.

Grit *and* **Sara** *go through the door.* **Jams** *stands uncertain. He goes to the door and shouts in the street.*

Jams   Keep her upright! You can't trust him to do – (*Yells.*) Don't let her stagger! O God get her round the corner before 'anyone – ! (*Whines.*) They're opening their doors! (*Shuts the door.*) I can't look!

He goes to the table. Sits. Drags the soup bowl towards him. Eats.

Chopped! That Johannson'll get my seat in the truck! Twisted little bed-wetter! (*Sobs.*) She brings crates into the house – then as if that's not enough – (*Shakes salt on the soup.*) – she kills herself! (*Eats. Splutters. Spits.*) O God what if she switched them round! . . . (*Collapses across the table. Weeps. Bangs the table with his fist.*) It's her revenge because I sat in her chair!

He gets up. Still howling he goes to the door, opens it and shouts into the street.

Leant! Leant – you bitch!

He groans at what he sees. Slams the door. He goes towards the kitchen, still howling.

Jams   O God it's worse than Reading.

Howling, he staggers towards the kitchen. There is a knock at the door. He turns and shouts to it.

Jams   Bugger off!

He goes off to the kitchen howling.